# Local Content in Procurement

Creating Local Jobs and Competitive Domestic Industries in Supply Chains

'Local content has become a key element in the strategic development of the extractive industry worldwide. This book is a highly recommended first-class guide by the foremost authority on the subject. Extraordinary clarity and insight have been combined to produce a must-have handbook for the serious international business executive and consultant.'

**Hon. Tam Brisibe, former Chairman, Committee of Petroleum Resources Upstream, House of Representatives, National Assembly, Nigeria**

'Local content has become a popular catchcry in many resource-rich countries. But while policy-makers are understandably eager to derive greater value-added benefits from the extraction of natural resources, formulating a regulatory framework for local content that will lead to the creation of internationally competitive domestic industries can be a fiendishly complex task. This clearly written book describes the pitfalls and outlines some of the solutions to this conundrum and should serve as a useful handbook to regulators and industry practitioners alike. '

**Joe Leahy, Brazil Bureau Chief, *Financial Times***

'What we have learned from this book is allowing us to focus on the practicalities of the local content in our invitations to tender for major contracts. We are now able to obtain tangible information and contractual commitments from tenderers to support our local content business objectives and be accountable to our stakeholders in Ghana.'

**Dinah Quashie-Idun, Local Content and Supplier Development Supervisor, Tullow Ghana Limited**

'A valuable book for all supply chain professionals living with local content challenges and opportunities. Always practical. Keep it close to your desk.'

**Simon Blamires, Regional Supply Chain Director, Africa, Newmont Mining, Ghana**

~~~~~~~~~~~~~~~~~~~~~

'This book is a first of its kind and a must-read for those working or in business in an overseas environment. Demonstrable local content is becoming a key to business success, provided the subject is fully understood and implemented with care. The author provides a practical approach with clear examples of how this success can be achieved.'

**Graham Balchin, Vice President of Projects, BG Trinidad and Tobago, Trinidad**

~~~~~~~~~~~~~~~~~~~~~

'The first comprehensive analysis of local content as a strategic factor, how it affects the ambitions of international businesses and how it can be turned into an opportunity. This is a book each business development, project and procurement manager should have on his desk.'

**Cesare Pagani, Human Resources and Local Content Manager, Heerema Marine Contractors, Angola**

~~~~~~~~~~~~~~~~~~~~~

'The book is a must-read for those of us responsible for formulating local content policy and regulations.'

**Elias A. Kilembe, Senior Principal Petroleum Geologist/Local Content Coordinator, Tanzania Petroleum Development Corporation**

~~~~~~~~~~~~~~~~~~~~~

'This book goes beyond mere lessons in local content, which it presents through practical examples and useful methodologies and tools. The book also offers deep reflection on local content as a fundamental strategy for procurement and how local content can be optimised to grow the economy of a country. Should this book be read? Absolutely!'

**François Bréant, Head of Industrial Strategy and Local Content Management, Total, Paris**

'In this book, Dr Michael Warner provides a holistic, comprehensive and practical framework for integrating local content into sourcing strategies. A timely and important contribution to understanding how local content in procurement may be leveraged for enabling the creation of local jobs and competitive domestic industries in supply chains.'

**Zanele Xuza, Preferential Procurement Manager, Anglo American**

'This book is a must-have for those who have responsibilities for formulating policies and strategies in government and the private sector on local content development. Well researched, it dwells in detail on the use of different local content models and emerging tools for bridging capacity gaps in the effective management of local content. In an area where there is still paucity of well-researched literature, this book fills a big gap, and not a moment too early.'

**Olamide Onasanya, Nigeria LNG Ltd, Head Nigerian Content Co-ordinator**

**Dr Michael Warner**

# Local Content in Procurement

## Creating Local Jobs and Competitive Domestic Industries in Supply Chains

Routledge
Taylor & Francis Group

LONDON AND NEW YORK

First published 2011 by Greenleaf Publishing Limited

Published 2017 by Routledge
2 Park Square, Milton Park, Abingdon, Oxon OX14 4RN
711 Third Avenue, New York, NY 10017, USA

*Routledge is an imprint of the Taylor & Francis Group, an informa business*

Cover by LaliAbril.com
Photo: Local welder engrossed in the construction of an offshore oil production platform at the TOFCO fabrication site in Trinidad and Tobago. Through a smart procurement strategy formulated by the investing oil company and a joint venture with an international contractor, execution of this contract in Trinidad achieved 91% local content and significantly enhanced the local firm's international competitiveness (see Chapter 4). Image by kind permission of TOFCO Ltd.

British Library Cataloguing in Publication Data:
    Warner, Michael.
        Local content in procurement : creating local jobs and
        competitive domestic industries in supply chains.
        1. Petroleum industry and trade--Materials management.
        2. Gas industry--Materials management. 3. Mineral
        industries--Materials management. 4. Economic development.
        5. Regional economics. 6. Social responsibility of
        business. 7. Job creation. 8. Contracting out.
        I. Title
        338.7'6223'0687-dc22

        ISBN-13: 978-1-906093-64-8 (hbk)

# Contents

# Acknowledgements

I wish to express my gratitude to certain individuals for their contribution to this book, be that of a conscious or unconscious nature: Mike Oakey, now a contracts engineer with BP, who kindly read through a number of the chapters in their early drafts; David Mottashed, my former manager and mentor in the contracts and procurement department at BG Group; Steve Ansell, former General Manager of the same function, and subsequent GMs Alistair Williams and Bill Nahill; Cyrille Putz, former Sustainable Development manager for Sodexo; Graham Balchin, who chaperoned a tour of the TOFCO fabrication yard in Trinidad along with Suresh Gangabissoon, its Managing Director; and Simon Maxwell, former Director of the Overseas Development Institute, who allowed me the room to wander about this subject for some years before venturing into corporate life. This book is also a testament to the willingness of many others to offer their perspective on the subject, including Steve Warner, Neil Cathmoir, Jamie Hamilton, Siobhan Woods, John Grant, Paul Burrell, Dirk William te Velde, Nick Gorton, Akan Odon, Sam Carroll, Dominic Hall, Clare Young, Barry Borhani, Petter Matthews, Matthew Lynch, Dave Savory and Mark Essex.

# Abbreviations

| | |
|---|---|
| AIP | Australian Industry Participation |
| APM | Association of Project Management, UK |
| ASME | American Society of Mechanical Engineers |
| AVC | actual value contributed |
| BEE | business enabling environment |
| BPTT | BP Trinidad and Tobago |
| CAPEX | capital expenditure |
| CDS | CDC Development Solutions |
| CIF | cost, insurance, freight |
| CIP | carriage and insurance paid |
| CPM | contractor management performance |
| DFID | Department for International Development, UK |
| DIISR | Department for Innovation, Industry, Science and Research, Australia |
| E&P | engineering and procurement |
| EIO | economic impact optimisation |
| EMS | environmental management system |
| EPBS | Enhanced Project Bylaws Scheme, Australia |
| EPC | engineering, procurement and construction |
| EPCm | engineering, procurement and construction-management |
| EPIC | engineering, procurement, installation and commissioning |
| ESIA | environmental and social impact assessment |
| EXW | ex-works/factory |
| FAC | first aid case |
| FEED | front-end engineering and design |
| FIDIC | International Federation of Consulting Engineers |
| FOB | free on board |
| FPAL | First Point Assessment Limited |
| FPSO | floating production, storage and offloading |
| FTE | full-time equivalent |

| | |
|---|---|
| G&G | geosciences and geophysics |
| GATS | General Agreement on Trade in Services |
| GATT | General Agreement on Tariffs and Trade |
| GDP | gross domestic product |
| GNI | gross national income |
| GNP | gross national product |
| GPA | Agreement on Government Procurement (WTO) |
| GRI | Global Reporting Initiative |
| HSE | health, safety and environment |
| HSSE | health, safety, security, environment |
| IBRD | International Bank for Reconstruction and Development |
| IDA | International Development Association |
| Incoterm | international commerce term |
| IRR | internal rate of return |
| IT | information technology |
| ITT | invitation to tender |
| JV | joint venture |
| LC | local content |
| LTIF | lost-time injury frequency |
| NAFTA | North American Free Trade Agreement |
| NCMA | North Coast Marine Area, Trinidad and Tobago |
| NJQS | NipeX Joint Qualification System |
| NPV | net present value |
| O&M | operations and maintenance |
| OECD | Organisation for Economic Co-operation and Development |
| OEM | original equipment manufacturer |
| OPEX | operational expenditure |
| PLCC | Permanent Local Content Committee, Trinidad and Tobago |
| QA | quality assurance |
| QC | quality control |
| R&D | research and development |
| RFP | request for proposal |
| RFQ | request for quote |
| scfd | standard cubic feet/day |
| SDT | special and differential treatment |
| SME | small-/medium-scale enterprise |
| SURF | subsea umbilicals risers and flowlines |
| T&T | Trinidad and Tobago |
| TRIF | total recordable incident frequency |
| TRIM | Trade-Related Investment Measure |
| UNDP | United Nations Development Programme |
| USAID | United States Agency for International Development |
| VAT | value-added tax |
| WTO | World Trade Organisation |

# Introduction

> This could be the largest private sector investment pro-
> gramme in the history of mankind—more than actually
> putting a man on the moon (Pedro Corderio, Head of Oil
> and Gas Practices for Bain & Company, São Paulo, in
> describing the US$1 trillion of investments planned for oil
> and gas development offshore of Brazil).[1]

Trillions of dollars of goods and services will be procured over the
next ten years in exploring and developing for oil, gas and mineral
resources around the globe. Over the same period more trillions of
dollars' worth of goods and services will be procured by public and
private companies and official development agencies to construct
water, power, buildings and transportation infrastructure and to
purchase associated manufactured equipment and components.[2]
But how much of this expenditure will be required to be discharged
through contracts with suppliers and subcontractors either resident
in, owned by, or tax-registered in the country in which this expenditure is to be invested? This is the trillion-dollar question on **local
content**.

1 J. Leahy, 'Platform for Growth', *Financial Times*, 16 March 2011: 11.
2 Annual expenditure on construction is estimated at US$7.5 trillion. Source:
  Global Construction Perspectives and Oxford Economics, 'Global Construction 2020: A Global Forecast', 2010; www.globalconstruction2020.
  com, accessed 9 June 2011.

The core thesis of this book is that large-scale procurement by private and public companies has been overlooked as a means to strategically and tactically develop national industries and generate employment. Procurement regulations, contracting strategies, vendor pre-qualification, technical standards, bid documents, tender evaluation criteria and contract conditions: all these instruments of procurement can be formulated creatively to build national competitiveness through capital investment, technology transfer and skills development.

More so than perhaps any other sectors, it is in investment in oil, gas and mineral development that the potential for procurement, and in particular tender procedures, to frame and incentivise local content is rising to the top of the political agenda. Local content regulators based within ministries of energy and mining and in nationally owned companies that partner with foreign investors, are watching each other closely. We are witnessing more and more stringent local content regulations appearing, directed at the procurement processes of oil, gas and mining companies, from Brazil to Ghana, Azerbaijan to Angola and Liberia to Kazakhstan. Whether this is good or bad, or legally or economically questionable, this *is* happening, and those involved in the formulation of these regulations, or in related matters of compliance, procurement, business development, project delivery or social performance, need to understand this phenomenon and its impact.

In particular, regulations for local content need to be formulated with great care. It is not inevitable, for example, that higher levels of local content invariably lead to economic benefits for the host economy. There are trade-offs to be understood here, not least what happens when local content levels reach the point where domestic suppliers are unable to win contracts on the basis of an internationally competitive tender. In such cases, the success of achieving local content targets in creating new jobs and filling local order books may be dampened by a concurrent deleterious impact on the country or region's long-term industrial competitiveness, or may introduce new risks and higher costs to investment projects, or even reduce the volume or timeliness of government revenues from these investments.

Alongside these questions on local content regulations sit corporate local content strategies and plans. These may be designed explicitly to comply with host country local content regulations, or they may be freestanding—a demonstration of a company's commitment to the national economy or local community, or part of the business development strategy of an international services contractor or equipment supplier.

An important principle in formulating both local content regulations and company local content strategies and plans, and one central to this book, is the golden thread that runs through the discipline of procurement, namely that contracts should be awarded or won on an internationally competitive basis. The attraction of this principle is that it sits at the fulcrum of public policy and commercial interests around local content. Policy-makers invariably want their economies to become internationally competitive, thereby to attract inward investment, sustain and grow the domestic job market and develop indigenous technologies. Likewise, commercially run public and private companies need to know that their procurement expenditure with domestic suppliers is being managed as efficiently as possible, and that prices, delivery times and quality are competitive with what could be secured if sourcing from foreign suppliers.

There are of course some very good reasons why, in the poorest economies, this principle of contract award on an internationally competitive basis might be temporarily and selectively waived, and these are discussed in this book. Yet the golden principle remains, providing a benchmark for determining the viability of new local content laws and regulations, and the efficacy of company local content strategies and investment plans.

## Overview of chapters

Those formulating local content regulations and company local content strategies and plans face a significant challenge. Will their interventions to leverage economic growth from procurement expenditure lead to more skilled and competitive domestic suppliers, or will they serve to perpetuate inefficient and uncompetitive national industries?

**Chapter 1: 'Competitiveness vs. protectionism'** applies a critical test to determine which local content regulations and local content strategies are likely to be protectionist: namely, does the regulation break the core principle that contracts be awarded on the basis of international competitiveness for price, quality and delivery? The chapter also forwards three arguments to justify why this principle might be temporarily and selectively suspended in emerging markets. These are the infant industry argument, the market power argument and an argument for social impact compensation.

Local content in the oil, gas and mining sectors is fast becoming a strategic factor in investment decision-making, project delivery and the formulation of public policy for industrial development. And yet investors, operating companies and public officials have few quantitative tools to inform dialogue over trade-offs or gauge the optimum levels of local content. **Chapter 2: 'Local content optimisation'** deploys economic impact optimisation modelling to demonstrate, for example, that introducing a mandatory local content target of 40% within a concession agreement negotiation may necessitate a reduction in royalty payments from 25% to 20% and a fall in corporation tax rates from 30% to 25%; or that, for project delivery, a 15% nominal price advantage to domestic suppliers increases local content in capital expenditure by 2.1% and employment by 7,500, but at a cost-premium of US$110 million, a loss of 0.4% in the internal rate of return for investors, and reduction in government life-cycle revenues of US$126 million.

Through an adaptation of the work of Peter Kraljic, **Chapter 3: 'Procurement strategy'** provides a basis for formulating procurement and contracting strategies that adjust to different capabilities, competitiveness and risk in the local supplier market. Three core components of procurement strategy are considered: the packaging of work (contract bundling versus unbundling), the level of client control in the supply chain, and the choice of compensation mechanism. Illustrations are given from Brazil and Trinidad and Tobago.

**Chapter 4: 'Case study'** offers a detailed example of how one leading multinational gas company, BG Group, adapted its procurement process to facilitate development of the competitiveness of a local contractor in Trinidad and Tobago. The local contractor, TOFCO Ltd, was contracted to fabricate and install the deck for a large platform, now producing from the Poinsettia field off the coast of Trinidad. The chapter is published with the kind permission of BG Group.

A high proportion of total expenditure on goods and services for major construction projects and operations is frequently procured through a small number of large contracts. **Chapter 5: 'Major contract tenders'** describes how to formulate invitations to tender and tender evaluation criteria for major contracts, with the aim of incentivising large international and domestic engineering and management services contractors to play a pivotal role in local content management.

Common barriers to accessing procurement opportunities for local small- and medium-scale enterprises (SMEs) are analysed in **Chapter 6: 'Accessible procurement'**. Different corporate procurement processes and procedures are described to improve this access, including clarity on the available opportunities, navigation of e-procurement, whether or not to relax pre-qualification criteria for nascent industries, and the key ingredients of a procurement communications plan for local SMEs.

**Chapter 7: 'SME development programmes'** is co-authored with Robert Webster of CDC Development Solutions, a respected SME capacity-building organisation whose clients have included the World Bank, USAID, BP, Exxon and Sonangol. Four key SME programme elements are considered: access to markets; technology and business processes; management and human capacity; and access to finance. The chapter emphasises the importance of local suppliers gaining pre-qualification certification and working in strategic partnerships with larger domestic and international suppliers in order to access higher-value procurement opportunities.

With local content regulations and aspirations being of particular relevance to underdeveloped countries, **Chapter 8: 'Aid procurement'** considers how procurement in aid programmes might follow the lead of the extractive industries so that, in the process of executing road, education, healthcare and other development projects, this aid concurrently stimulates private sector development through the creation of sustainable jobs and competitive suppliers within local supply chains.

The mandatory definitions and reporting requirements of state regulators, and the voluntary metrics and reporting standards of companies, vary widely: from crude measures such as the country address on an invoice, to verified certificates proving that goods are of domestic origin. **Chapter 9: 'Metrics and measurement'** unpacks the complexities of different metrics for reporting local content and assesses their advantages and disadvantages. Comparison is also made between how Brazil and Kazakhstan use rules of origin methods to measure local content. The chapter also draws attention to important missing metrics.

## Strategies for managing local content

It is perhaps worth noting the obvious: that the formulation of procurement procedures and processes is but one approach to managing local content. The formulation of state laws and regulations on local content as well as public investments in business-friendly infrastructure and fiscal incentive also have their place, and often set the foundations for successful procurement-based strategies. Likewise, well-crafted corporate local content standards and country-level local content strategies and plans also play their part, and often foresee a role for procurement practices alongside innovative engineering and design, a focus on staff recruitment and training, and targeted social investment and community-based supplier development programmes.

Then there is the question of the size of the local market. Attracting new capital investment from international contractors and equipment manufacturers into the domestic economy is essentially a commercial decision, predicated on anticipated revenues and other market demand factors. And, yet, sometimes all that is on offer is a one-off contract for an isolated investment project. Local content regulations or company local content strategies that compel lead contractors to make investments in such circumstances are unlikely to satisfy any of the key parties. The solution lies in part in an aggregation of demand within and across sectors within the country, and in part in regional trade regimes that create sufficiently large markets that such investments become commercially viable. This in turn requires collaboration between investors and/or among regional governments, which requires those who have the geopolitical power to facilitate agreement between the relevant parties.

As can be seen, then, the topic of local content is wide, and although this book addresses many of the relevant areas, in particular around procurement, regulation and strategy, some important local content topics are not covered herein. These include, but are not limited to:

- The nationalisation of direct employment and progression of nationals into supervisor and management positions

- The participation of national equity in inward investment, development of concessions and domestic supply chains

- The role of **competition and anti-discrimination law** in defining what can and cannot be realised within procurement to mandate or incentivise local content and local supplier development

- The role of **environmental, social and economic impact assessment studies** as a vehicle for identifying opportunities to enhance local content and develop local suppliers

- How to drive **community content** (what some refer to as 'local local' content) through operations and maintenance contracts, including incentives for building inclusive business models and incubating local enterprises within international contracts

- How public and private corporations might go about modifying their **policies**, **organisational structure** and resourcing in order to effectively manage local content

- The **role of the public sector** in providing the incentives and investment to support local content and supplier development

- The geopolitics and corporate realities of building **regional markets** sufficiently large to attract inward investment from international manufacturers and services contractors

- How local content compliance regulations and corporate strategies developed primarily for the oil and gas sector are now being adopted in **other sectors**, such as utilities and infrastructure

These and other topics may be perhaps the subject of a sequel to this book.


# Definition of local content

The term 'local content' needs defining. First is to define the total volume of procurement expenditure within which lies the subset of local content. In the book, this subset is taken to include both the 'thin end' and the 'thick end' of the wedge of a company's total procurement expenditure: that is, both minor and major contracts.

Second is to define how far down the supply chain to look. Again, this book takes a broad perspective and includes both direct procurement of local goods and services by the parent company, as well as indirect procurement of local goods and services by higher-tier local or foreign suppliers.

Third is to define local content itself. Unless otherwise stated, the term is used throughout this book to mean more than just the proportion of contract value going on goods and services of domestic origin (or some other measure of 'local'). Instead it is interpreted to mean the **composite value contributed to the national economy from the purchase of bought-in goods and services**, and includes wages and benefits, materials, equipment and plant, subcontracts and taxes. It also includes first-order, direct economic impacts on the national employees of contractors and suppliers, second-order, indirect impacts on their suppliers and subcontractors and sub-subcontractors, and third-order, induced impacts arising as the income earned by nationals and resident workers is spent in the wider domestic economy.

Finally, local content is taken here to mean 'national'. It includes the proportion of a company's procurement expenditure with community-based suppliers or suppliers who source labour or materials from local affected communities, as well as procurement from larger, nationally operating local or foreign suppliers (what is sometimes referred to as 'national content' or 'national industry participation'), and also from foreign suppliers who source certain goods and services from the local market.

Given the obvious complexity in using the term 'local content' and the myriad of definitions, perhaps some kindly advice might be to recommend that when discussing local content try not to use this term at all. Instead, simply say exactly what it is you mean. Chapter 9 offers 53 ways to do this.

# 1

# Competitiveness vs. protectionism

## Is local content a road to economic competitiveness or a pathway to protectionism?

## The problem

In January 2011, the *Folha de São Paulo* newspaper in Brazil reported that Petrobras—the state-owned international oil company—might consider reducing its expenditure on locally produced content in the supply of goods and services from 65% to 35%.[1] This claim was rapidly refuted by the company.[2] The incident demonstrates the

1 upstreamonline.com, 'Petrobras eyes lower local content', Folha de São Paulo, 24 January 2011; www.upstreamonline.com/live/article242378. ece, accessed 24 January 2011.
2 *Offshore Energy Today*, 'Brazil: Petrobras Rebuffs Claims it Plans to Slash Local Equipment Purchases', 25 January 2011; www.offshoreenergytoday. com/brazil-petrobras-rebuffs-claims-it-plans-to-slash-local-equipment-purchases, accessed 30 January 2011.

tensions that can exist around local content targets, and the question of whether they are a rational public policy for development of nascent or re-emergent domestic industries, or on occasions excessive and represent a form of unjustified protectionism.

Of course, it is not the setting of local content targets per se that carries the potential for protectionism. It is whether the targets themselves might lead to levels of local procurement that exceed the capability of national suppliers to win work on an internationally competitive basis. The basis for setting local content targets is a choice between options. Either targets are established within the capabilities of domestic suppliers to win orders or service contracts against international competition; or, targets are set knowing that local suppliers are not sufficiently competitive to win contracts on a level playing field, but that this is deemed justifiable as a public policy in order to protect domestic industry, create local jobs or develop local capabilities over time. Alternatively, regulatory authorities may genuinely (or disingenuously) believe that targets are being set on an internationally competitive basis, when in reality this is not the case.

## Defining competitiveness and protectionism

It would be helpful at this juncture to define what is meant by international competitiveness and protectionism as these terms relate to local content in the procurement of goods and services in the oil and gas industry. In this book we consider *competitiveness* as a comparative concept, specifically: the ability of a domestic supplier or contractor to supply goods or services in an international market. Importantly, this market could be entirely within the domestic economy, with foreign and local firms competing against each other in open competition. Or, it can mean a market in a foreign country accessible to domestic suppliers.

The term *protectionism* refers to the intended or unintended economic policy of restraining trade between countries through methods such as tariffs (taxes) on imported goods, or restrictive import quotas and regulations designed to discourage imports. The setting of local content targets would fall within the category of restrictive import quotas. Regulations that give preference to domestic suppliers over foreign suppliers (e.g. through domestic-only tender lists or price advantages to local suppliers) could be deemed a form of import discouragement.

Under World Trade Organisation rules for Trade-Related Investment Measures (TRIMs), local content measures are explicitly prohibited if these oblige the purchase or use by an enterprise of products of domestic origin or from a domestic source, whether this is specified in terms of particular products, the volume or value of products, or in terms of a proportion of volume or value of local production. Similar prohibitions are contained in pan-regional and bilateral trade agreements.

This interpretation of protectionism as an anticompetitive obligation on an individual firm suggests the need for some further refinement of the aforementioned definition for competitiveness. The World Economic Forum refers in its annual Competitiveness Report to 'national competitiveness', and includes in this definition not only the capability of domestic firms in terms of their business sophistication and technological readiness to penetrate foreign markets and compete with imports in the domestic market, but also the competitiveness of the nation state as a whole: for example, the quality of its education system and training institutions, extent of physical infrastructure, degree of macroeconomic stability and the general health of its citizens.

Table 1.1 compares the national competitiveness of oil- and gas-producing countries against the top 12 most competitive countries. (This ranking is based on a composite weighted average, and the reader is advised to refer to the detailed report for rankings associated with the different criteria on firm competitiveness.)

Whether looking at international competitiveness through the lens of the individual firm, or the economic and industrial characteristics of an entire nation, an important test of a nation's competitiveness is whether domestic suppliers are able to win work in international markets on a competitive basis. In other words, if engaged in a full and fair process of contractor selection, are domestic suppliers able to beat the competition to win contracts?

Table 1.1 **Global competitiveness index ranking, 2010 to 2012, oil- and gas-producing countries**

Source: World Economic Forum, *The Global Competitiveness Report 2010–2011* (Geneva: World Economic Forum, 2010): 15, Table 4.

| Top 12 rankings | | Ranking of oil- and gas-producing countries (out of 139) | | | |
|---|---|---|---|---|---|
| Switzerland | 1 | Norway | 14 | Vietnam | 59 |
| Sweden | 2 | Australia | 16 | Turkey | 61 |
| Singapore | 3 | Qatar | 17 | Russian Federation | 63 |
| United States | 4 | Saudi Arabia | 21 | Mexico | 66 |
| Germany | 5 | UAE | 25 | Romania | 67 |
| Japan | 6 | Malaysia | 26 | Colombia | 68 |
| Finland | 7 | China | 27 | Iran | 69 |
| Netherlands | 8 | Brunei | 28 | Kazakhstan | 72 |
| Denmark | 9 | Tunisia | 32 | Peru | 73 |
| Canada | 10 | Oman | 34 | Egypt | 81 |
| Hong Kong SAR | 11 | Kuwait | 35 | Trinidad and Tobago | 84 |
| United Kingdom | 12 | Thailand | 38 | Philippines | 85 |
| | | Indonesia | 44 | Algeria | 86 |
| | | Italy | 48 | Argentina | 87 |
| | | India | 51 | Syria | 97 |
| | | Azerbaijan | 57 | Libya | 100 |
| | | Brazil | 58 | Ecuador | 105 |
| | | | | Ghana | 114 |
| | | | | Venezuela | 122 |
| | | | | Nigeria | 127 |
| | | | | Timor-Leste | 133 |
| | | | | Angola | 138 |
| | | | | Chad | 139 |
| | | | | Gabon | x |
| | | | | Yemen | x |
| | | | | Republic of Congo | x |
| | | | | Equatorial Guinea | x |
| | | | | Iraq | x |
| | | | | Sudan | x |
| | | | | São Tomé & Príncipe | x |

Whether a process of contractor selection can ever be truly 'full' and 'fair' is of course open to challenge. Even if the contract award process itself is genuinely competitive, with pre-qualification and tender evaluation processes applied equally to all prospective bidders, and contracts awarded strictly on tender submissions, there is still the question of the advantages and disadvantages that lie outside of the immediate control of the supplier.

For example, foreign and domestic vendors may be exposed to very different tax regimes. A prospective foreign supplier may be subject to import tariffs and withholding tax, which disadvantages its price competitiveness. But then a domestic supplier may be disadvantaged because of local value added tax that is not applicable to the foreign supplier. The USA, for example, does not participate in a VAT system, and can argue that it is disadvantaged when exporting equipment to countries that then add this type of tax to the sales price.

Conversely, a foreign supplier may be advantaged by export subsidies from its own government, such as export credit guarantees, or by a public policy of the host government to attract inward investment through relief on import duties. Likewise, local suppliers may benefit from access to subsidised sources of domestic credit: for example, from national development banks, or from subsidised energy costs.

These competitive externalities are difficult to overcome, which is why they often form key themes within international and bilateral trade negotiations.

There are also concealed advantages at the firm level, as well as the national level. Price competitiveness is one area of obvious scrutiny. Figure 1.1 compares all-inclusive labour rates across a sample of countries. On the face of it, the figure suggests that labour rates in Nigeria are more competitive than in the US (Gulf Coast). But this is misleading, since labour rates, even if 'all-inclusive', are not always reflective of a firm's price competitiveness.

Figure 1.1 **Comparison of labour rate competitiveness across countries**

Source: Compass, *The 2010 Construction Cost and Reference Yearbook* (Pennsylvania: Compass International Consultants Inc, 10th annual edition, 2010).

**Labour hour rates (skilled, high-end, all-inclusive)**

Comparative labour productivity—the ratio of output to labour input—is a more meaningful measure of competitiveness, reflecting the overall efficiency of workers in producing a unit of output that meets the required quality standards. Labour productivity is influenced by many factors that lie outside the workers' direct influence and outside the all-inclusive labour rate. This includes the amount of capital equipment available to workers, the presence of new, more

Figure 1.2 **Comparison of labour productivity across countries**

Source: Compass, *The 2010 Construction Cost and Reference Yearbook* (Pennsylvania: Compass International Consultants Inc, 10th annual edition, 2010).

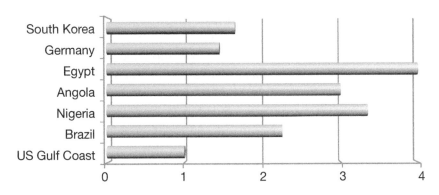

**Construction labour productivity ('poor' case)**

efficient technologies, and the quality and sophistication of management practices. Figure 1.2 contrasts the same countries by labour productivity. This figure suggests that in Nigeria construction projects may take up to 3.35 times more labour to produce the same output unit compared with the US Gulf Coast.

# The golden thread through procurement

These externalities (though less so the concealed internalities) are sometimes used by oil-, gas- and mineral-producing countries to justify protectionist local content regulations. But whether they can also justify regulations that undermine a fair and competitive process of contractor selection within procurement is questionable.

In the oil, gas and mining sectors, procurement departments go to great lengths to assure that tender alerts, pre-qualification criteria, choice of tenderers, instructions to tenders and tender evaluation criteria, are equally applied to all capable vendors. Throughout the process of contractor selection, it is the rule of 'comparative advantage' that pervades key decisions and assures contracts are awarded on a competitive basis. This, then, is the key principle of procurement—the *golden thread*—that runs through all regulations on local content, and assures that the award of contracts to domestic suppliers is free of explicit protection.

The principle is codified in the oil and gas development industry through clauses in articles within concession agreements or production-sharing agreements, and in mining through various forms of mining development agreements. These clauses then feed through into agreed tender procedures at the operational level.

Box 1.1 presents the typical clauses. What these provisions are essentially saying is that only when all else is equal should the buyer advantage domestic suppliers, and that in so doing the core principle of contract award on an internationally competitive basis is preserved.

Box 1.1 **Common clauses aligning local preferencing to the principle of competitive contract award**

Typical clause on competitive procurement in production-sharing agreement for oil and gas exploration and development:

> Give preference to local contractors and locally manufactured materials and equipment so long as their performance, quality and time of delivery are competitive with international performance and prices.

Typical clause on competitive procurement in a mining development agreement:[a]

> The Company shall, when purchasing goods and services required with respect to Mining Operations, give first preference, at comparable quality, delivery schedule and price, to goods produced in [COUNTRY] and services provided by [COUNTRY] citizens or businesses, subject to technical acceptability and availability of the relevant goods and services in [COUNTRY].

a   International Bar Association, 'Model Mining Development Agreement'; www.mmdaproject.org, 2010, accessed 9 June 2011

In practice, to argue that such clauses give preference to domestic suppliers is perhaps a little disingenuous. To 'give preference so long as competitive with international performance and price', is to require the domestic supplier to meet minimum technical performance requirements and then also equal its international rivals on price. As such, the domestic supplier could be awarded the contract with, or without, the stated preference. (The maths is slightly different for contracts awarded on a 'value for money' basis, but the same core principle and outcome still applies.)

What such a clause does do, however, is suggest which categories of expenditure are likely to be excluded from participation by domestic suppliers. This includes goods and services:

- Of a proprietary nature—sometimes called 'exotic' goods—unless domestic distributors are appointed

- Strategic to the functioning of operations on the grounds of schedule (e.g. long-led items) or health and safety

page 21 ➜

**Table 1.2 Adherence of local content regulations to the principle of competitive contract award**

| Typology of local content regulations | Adheres to principle of competitive contract award (Yes/No) |
|---|---|
| **Minimum targets** | |
| Blanket minimum local content targets—intentionally exceeds price competitiveness of domestic supplier industry in order to drive inward investment | No/Yes (in some sub-categories of expenditure local suppliers will be competitive, in others not) |
| Disaggregated minimum local content targets—in each case exceeding price competitiveness of domestic suppliers in order to drive inward investment | No (but converging on 'Yes' if inward investment is forthcoming and successful in driving domestic competitiveness) |
| Disaggregated minimum local content targets for expenditure—within domestic limits of international price competitiveness | Yes |
| **Local supplier preferences** | |
| Domestic-only tender lists—benchmarked against 'capability', but not internationally competitive on price, quality and delivery | No |
| Domestic-only tender lists—benchmarked against international competitiveness | Yes |
| Full, fair and reasonable access to procurement opportunities for domestic suppliers | Yes |

| Typology of local content regulations | Adheres to principle of competitive contract award (Yes/No) |
|---|---|
| Reduced pre-qualification criteria for domestic suppliers | Yes (does not necessarily imply contract award on an uncompetitive basis) |
| Mandated foreign/domestic consortia or subcontractor alliances | Yes/No ('Yes' if presence of foreign suppliers assures whole of bid is internationally competitive, e.g. through additional supervision, training or upfront investment, with these costs offset by savings in labour costs and logistics. 'No' if leads to net cost escalation) |
| Minimum participation of domestic subcontractors/suppliers in contracts awarded to foreign suppliers (by $ value) | No (if this leads to uncompetitive pricing) |
| Minimum national ownership of suppliers awarded contracts | No (if this leads to uncompetitive pricing) |
| **Basis of contract award** | |
| Preference to domestic suppliers so long as performance, quality and time of delivery are competitive with international performance and prices | Yes |
| Nominal price advantage to domestic suppliers on award, e.g. 10% blanket | No |

| Typology of local content regulations | Adheres to principle of competitive contract award (Yes/No) |
|---|---|
| Bid evaluation on basis of 'where all else equal, preference local suppliers or highest levels of local content' | Yes |
| Economically advantageous basis for contract award, e.g. application of 'K' Factor | Yes (if applied equally to all bidders) |
| Contract award veto for government authorities on tender board on basis of insufficient local content or inadequate local content plan | No (if veto is applied to detriment of principle of contract award on an internationally competitive basis) |
| **Contract execution** | |
| Advance payments to domestic suppliers, e.g. 30% | No (need for advance payment is indicator of supplier having insufficient cash flow or access to credit) |
| Minimum training obligations for nationals, e.g. first consideration to nationals, targets by cost or training hours | Yes (a form of 'offset' applied equally to all bidders) |
| Minimum obligations for growing competitiveness of domestic suppliers, e.g. minimum investment requirements, minimum training obligations beyond that needed for contract execution | Yes (a form of 'offset' applied equally to all bidders) |
| Obligations to report on local content performance | Yes (if not tied to mandatory minimum targets that breach domestic competitiveness) |

- That are one-offs or procured on an indeterminate ad hoc basis, and which if procured locally would incur prohibitively high transaction costs

Table 1.2 contrasts different local content regulations in terms of their adherence to the principle of contract award on an internationally competitive basis.

Those regulations most at odds with the core principle include local content targets that breach the capacities and price competitiveness of domestic industry; requirements for minimum levels of participation by domestic suppliers in international contracts or participation of domestic firms owned by nationals; and the granting of a nominal price advantage to domestic suppliers.

## Arguments for protectionism

The types of regulation in Table 1.2 are commonly justified by host governments with reference to established economic arguments.

Specifically, those regulations that compel contracts to be awarded on a non-competitive basis may in fact have an economic or social rationale. Three of the most common arguments are the **infant industry** argument, the **market power** argument and what might be described as the **social impact** argument. These are discussed in turn below.

### Infant industry argument

The infant industry argument was first espoused by Alexander Hamilton, a Founding Father of the United States and Secretary of the Treasury. Hamilton was an advocate of government intervention to support business in a fledgling country, and a strong opponent of free trade.[3] The same argument continues today in many emerging and developing economies. The argument asserts that protectionism is acceptable where nascent industries do not yet have the

---

3  Wikipedia, 'Alexander Hamilton'; en.wikipedia.org/wiki/
   Alexander_Hamilton, accessed 16 February 2011.

Figure 1.3 **Infant industry argument**

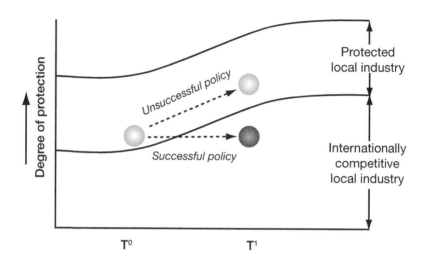

economies of scale of foreign competitors, and thus need support (protection) until such a time as they can attain a similar level of competitiveness.

Figure 1.3 is a schematic showing how, under the infant industry argument, limited protectionism is intended to lead over time to a domestic industry able to compete against international trade. It also shows what happens if the efforts of governments to intervene through education, training, sourcing preferences, capital investment, tax incentives and so on are unsuccessful (what is referred to as 'double market failure'; see Box 1.2 for definition).

Box 1.2 **Double market failure**

Double market failure is the failure of government interventions to correct failures in the free market.[a]

An example of double market failure would be local content regulations that preference domestic suppliers over foreign suppliers in an effort to correct the 'unfair' global purchasing power of international suppliers, but which then has the unintended effect of entrenching production inefficiencies and contributing further to an internationally uncompetitive domestic industry.

a   R. Zerbe and H. McCurdy, 'The End of Market Failure', *Regulation Journal* 23.2 (2000; www.cato.org/pubs/regulation/regv23n2/zerbe.pdf).

While this policy has benefited many countries, not least the United States, it has also been shown to be less than effective, with the result being inflation of the domestic products in question and lower quality, coupled with a failure of these firms to penetrate export markets.

To illustrate, during the 1980s, Brazil imposed controls on the import of computers with the intention of nurturing its own computer industry. This industry never materialised, with domestic production copying low-technology foreign computers sold at inflated prices.[4]

But the infant argument is by no means obsolete. Indeed, only recently the Financing for Development initiative of the United Nations argued for limited, time-bound protection of certain industries by countries in the early stages of industrialisation, noting that 'however misguided the old model of blanket protection intended to nurture import substitute industries, it would be a mistake to go to the other extreme and deny developing countries the opportunity of actively nurturing the development of an industrial sector'.[5]

Referring back to Table 1.2, certain local content regulations are more likely than others to lead to double market failure: that is, the unintended fuelling of inefficient and uncompetitive domestic industries. For example, regulations that limit contracts for certain sub-categories of expenditure to the preserve of 100% nationally owned companies, would, if such companies were currently uncompetitive and unable to attract new investment or benefit from technology transfer, be likely to fail the infant industry argument.

In contrast, regulations that limited the proportion of foreign content in certain expenditure, but concurrently encouraged foreign companies to form joint ventures with local firms, might stand a greater chance of fulfilling the infant industry argument. A case in point is the development of the TOFCO Ltd fabrication yard in

4  L. Eduardo, *The Microcomputer Industry in Brazil: The Case of a Protected High-Technology Industry* (Santa Barbara, CA: Greenwood Publishing, 1996).
5  E. Zedillo, 'Report of the High-Level Panel on Financing for Development'; www.un.org/reports/financing/full_report.pdf, 2001: 9, accessed 9 June 2011.

Trinidad and Tobago. (Full details of this case are described in Chapter 4.)

In this case, encouraged by a general industrial policy of local participation by nationally owned firms, and supported by a specific public policy on local content that encouraged oil and gas companies to develop local capability and competitiveness,[6] BP Trinidad and Tobago contracted the TOFCO fabrication yard to construct a series of offshore platforms. The protectionist component took the form of premiums, which elevated the cost of local fabrication above what might have been achieved through international competition. The first of the series of similar-specification platforms—the Cannonball project—received a premium of US$9 million, from a total cost of US$54 million.[7]

The combination of public policy and strategic procurement by BP can be considered a successful market intervention. Over time, as productivity in the fabrication yard improved, the premiums for subsequent platforms were able to be reduced. By the third platform, another foreign operator in the country—BG Group—was able to procure the services of TOFCO to construct a far larger platform. This time contract award was on a fully internationally competitive basis for cost, quality and schedule. Subsequently, the overall project—the Poinsettia project—won the Overseas Project of the Year Award 2009 from the UK-based Association of Project Management (APM). Justification for the award cited the contribution of the project to developing the fabrication industry in Trinidad as a deciding factor. As recorded by the General Manger of TOFCO, Suresh Gangabissoon, at the award ceremony, the contract 'raised the capability of TOFCO and local companies to an altogether higher, more competitive level'.[8]

---

6  Government of Trinidad and Tobago, 'Local Content and Local Participation Policy Framework', Ministry of Energy and Energy Industries, Permanent Local Content Committee; www.energy.gov.tt, 2005, accessed 9 June 2011.

7  Arthur Lok Jack Graduate School of Business, University of the West Indies, 'BP Trinidad and Tobago Limited', 2005, MCS-CSR-05-05; https://www.menas.co.uk/App_Data/elib/bptt.pdf, accessed 22 June 2011.

8  Rigzone, 'Poinsettia Project Honored as "Overseas Project of the Year" '; www.rigzone.com/news/article.asp?a_id=82055, 2009, accessed 17 February 2011.

Figure 1.4 **Realisation of the infant industry argument in Trinidad**

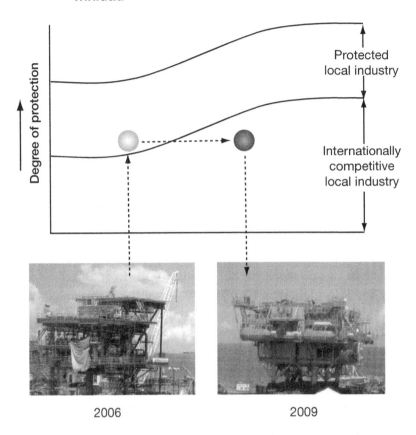

Figure 1.4 offers a schematic showing how the aforementioned BP platforms constructed in Trinidad paved the way for the nascent local fabricator to build its competitiveness over a finite time period.

## Market power argument

A second rationale for justifying protectionist local content regulations is where foreign suppliers are charged to be unfairly using market power to compete with domestic industry. From one viewpoint, this is simply an extension of the infant industry argument, in that if domestic companies could achieve the same purchasing power as international suppliers, then they too could negotiate the same global sourcing arrangements to compete on price. But there is a difference here. Whereas under the infant industry argument, local content targets and local preferencing regulations seek to advantage domestic industry, under the market power argument local content regulations are designed, not to 'advantage' local industry, but to ensure that this industry is not 'disadvantaged'.

The policy rationale is that the market power of some international suppliers means they inadvertently behave in an anticompetitive manner. This charge most commonly arises when international contractors commit to long-term global sourcing deals and bulk purchases to supply their large portfolio of clients around the world. These commitments and volumes enable the negotiation of substantially lower pricing. Such deals might be viewed as anticompetitive if they disadvantage capable domestic suppliers, who, given the opportunity to bid directly and individually against these global suppliers, might be able to compete. Of course, the domestic suppliers are unlikely to be competitive on base price, since they would have insufficient capacity to negotiate the same bulk deals. But their geography and lower labour costs may well mean they are more competitive on delivery, reliability and on total outturn cost: for example, if factoring in logistics costs and labour costs in repair and maintenance services.

Just such a scenario was played out recently in Queensland, Australia, in the context of a number of large liquid natural gas projects (see Box 1.3).

Box 1.3 **Local content regulations based on the market power argument, Queensland, Australia**

As a member of the World Trade Organisation, Australia carries obligations on competitiveness and anti-discrimination. Project proponents in Australia are prohibited from preferencing domestic suppliers over foreign suppliers, and may not instruct a first-tier supplier to use particular domestic suppliers or subcontractors as a condition of doing business.

However, in recognition of the market power argument (see main text), project proponents must adhere to the Australian Industry Participation National Framework[a] when procuring goods and services. The Framework is a policy for ensuring full, fair and reasonable opportunity for Australian industries to participate in significant public and private sector activity. The core definitions are as follows:

- **Full.** Domestic industry has the same opportunity afforded to other global supply chain partners to participate in all aspects of an investment project (e.g. design, engineering, project management, professional services, IT architecture)
- **Fair**. Domestic industry is provided the same opportunity as global suppliers to compete on investment projects on an equal and transparent basis, including being given reasonable time in which to tender
- **Reasonable**. Tenders are free from non-market burdens that might rule out domestic industry and are structured in such a way as to provide domestic industries the opportunity to participate in investment projects

To operationalise the Framework, project proponents are incentivised through the Enhanced Project Bylaws Scheme (EPBS), whereby goods that are not deemed to be manufactured in Australia may be imported and eligible for a 5% tariff relief. The scheme is administered by AusIndustry, part of the Department for Innovation, Industry, Science and Research (DIISR). Eligibility for tariff relief is predicated on approval of an Australian Industry Participation Plan (AIP Plan) in accordance with the Australian Industry Participation National Framework.

To gain approval for an AIP Plan, evidence is required demonstrating that consultation has taken place to determine whether there are Australian manufacturers capable of participating in tenders to supply the required goods. To this end, AusIndustry encourages project proponents to work with the quasi-government organisation, Industry Capability Network. Criteria to be satisfied in the approval of an AIP Plan, includes details of:[b]

- Employment creation
- Skills transfer
- Regional economic development
- Technology transfer and R&D
- Full, fair and reasonable opportunities for Australian suppliers to tender
- Strategic partnering and consortia building
- Integration of domestic suppliers into global supply chains
- Adoption of global best practice standards

a   Commonwealth Government, 'Australian Industry Participation National Framework', DIISR; www.innovation.gov.au/Industry/AustralianIndustryParticipation/Pages/AustralianIndustryParticipationNationalFramework.aspx, 2001, accessed 9 June 2011.
b   AusIndustry, 'Enhanced Project By-law Scheme: Policy and Administrative Guidelines', April 2010; www.ausindustry.gov.au/ImportandExport/EnhancedProjectBy-lawSchemeEPBS/Documents/EPBS%20-%20Policy%20and%20Administrative%20Guidelines%20-%20APR10.pdf, accessed 22 June 2011.

## Social impact argument

A third argument for imposing protectionist local content regulations is as a form of compensation for the adverse socioeconomic impacts of oil, gas and mining investment on local communities and vulnerable groups.

The regulatory requirements of ministries of environment for environmental impact assessment studies, and similarly those of development finance institutions and commercial banks, increasingly recognise that communities close to infrastructure projects may need to be compensated for a temporary or permanent loss of economic livelihoods. Preferencing employment and procurement opportunities to these individuals and to community-based vendors can play a part in this compensation.

The international benchmark standards for environmental and social impact assessment are the Performance Standards of the International Finance Corporation[9] (the private sector arm of the World Bank Group). These standards, adopted by over 60 commercial banks, including Citigroup and Barclays, provide principles for compensating individuals for the loss of potential to earn an income. Among the principles are compensation and benefits for:

- Persons physically displaced by an investment project, including 'assistance to help them improve or at least restore their standards of living or livelihoods', and 'opportunities to displaced persons and communities to derive appropriate development benefits from the project'

- Persons economically displaced, including additional 'targeted assistance (e.g. credit facilities, training or job opportunities) and opportunities to improve or at least restore their income-earning capacity, production levels, and standards of living'

In practice, this could involve project proponents directly tendering opportunities to suppliers who source labour or materials from affected communities, or it could mean obliging their major

---

9 International Finance Corporation, *Social and Environmental Performance Standards* (Washington, DC: IFC, 2006).

contractors to meet targets for employment of displaced and affected persons.

This type of local preferencing may be covenanted as part of the approval of environmental and social management plans by regulatory authorities, or it may be an entirely voluntarily undertaking by the company. For example, regarding the latter, it could be undertaken as a means to support permitting applications to local government authorities, or as a form of *soft* security—local goodwill affording the company and its workers protection from local hostilities.

# World Trade Organisation rules

Determining whether or not countries are justified in applying protectionist measures to domestic expenditure on goods and services is a key part of the mandate of the World Trade Organisation. The WTO describes itself as 'the only global international organization dealing with the rules of trade between nations. At its heart are the WTO agreements, negotiated and signed by the bulk of the world's trading nations and ratified in their parliaments.'[10]

Three of the most relevant agreements of WTO members with implications for local content regulations are the agreement on Trade-Related Investment Measures (TRIMs), the General Agreement on Trade in Services (GATS) and the agreement on Government Procurement (GPA). Each is discussed in turn below.

### TRIMs Agreement

The TRIMs Agreement is Article III of the General Agreement on Tariffs and Trade and is an agreement pertaining to trade in goods. It applies to all WTO members; that is, it is 'multilateral'. The rules under the TRIMs Agreement prohibit local content requirements that oblige particular levels of local procurement by an enterprise.

---

10 WTO, 'What is the WTO?'; www.wto.org/english/thewto_e/whatis_e/ whatis_e.htm, accessed 23 February 2011.

The rules also prohibit trade-balancing requirements that restrict the volume or value of imports that an enterprise can purchase to an amount related to the level of products it exports. In essence, the rules require a host country to extend to foreign investors treatment that is at least as favourable as the treatment it accords to national investors in like circumstances.

Importantly, the Agreement contains transitional arrangements. These allow WTO members to maintain certain (protectionist) measures for a limited time following their entry to the WTO. The period of grace is two years in the case of developed country members, five years for developing country members and seven years for least-developed country members.

As of 2011, of the 153 WTO members, 27 are developing-country oil or gas producers, with another three producers classified as least developed countries.[11] Of the 27, all except Vietnam acceded to the WTO prior to 2006, which would suggest that their eligibility for transitional arrangements under GATT have expired. The same is so for the three least developing countries—Angola, Chad and the Republic of Congo—who all acceded prior to 2004.

Notwithstanding extensions to the transitional arrangements under the ongoing Doha Round, or negotiated exemptions for committed sub-sectors, it is at least questionable whether governments who continue to apply local content requirements that afford protection to their domestic industries might be in breach of their obligations under the WTO. For example, questions have been raised recently about the Nigerian Oil & Gas Industry Content Development Act 2010 (the 'Local Content Act').[12] In this case, should a foreign company conducting business in Nigeria, or another WTO country member, raise this issue through the WTO dispute settlement facility, it seems likely that the Nigerian Government would proffer the infant industry or market power arguments in its defence.

---

11  WTO, 'Members and Observers'; www.wto.org/english/thewto_e/whatis_e/tif_e/org6_e.htm, accessed 23 February 2011.

12  A. Oni, 'The Local Content Act: A Breach of Nigeria's WTO Obligations', Business Day, 1 December 2010; www.businessdayonline.com/NG/index.php/law/legal-culture/16459-the-local-content-act-a-breach-of-nigerias-wto-obligations-, accessed 25 February 2011.

## General Agreement on Trade in Services

With regard to services as opposed to goods, Part III of the General Agreement on Trade in Services (GATS) contains provisions on access for foreign suppliers to WTO member markets ('market access') and the treatment of national suppliers ('national treatment').

In the case of **market access**, all WTO members should accord services and service providers from other WTO members treatment no less favourable than that provided for under the common terms, limitations and conditions mutually agreed within the WTO. The intention of this provision is to progressively eliminate certain types of protectionist measure, including limitations on:

- Numbers of foreign service providers allowed to compete with domestic providers
- The total value of service transactions of foreign providers
- The total number of foreign service operations or foreign people employed
- The type of legal entity or joint venture through which a service is provided
- Maximum levels of foreign capital participation

In the case of the rules for **national treatment**, the objective of the WTO here is to oblige member countries to treat foreign service suppliers and domestic service suppliers in the same manner.

As with GATT, under GATS there are provisions for the 'special and differential treatment' of developing countries (SDTs). These provisions include:

- Longer time periods for implementing agreements
- Measures to increase trading opportunities for these countries
- Provisions requiring all WTO members to safeguard the trade interests of developing countries
- Support to help developing countries build the infrastructure for WTO work, including handling disputes and implementing technical standards

## Box 1.4 **Offset transactions**

Offset transactions are contractual conditions that require the seller (usually a foreign supplier) to transfer additional economic benefits to the buyer (usually a host government or domestic company) as a condition for the sale of a base good or service.[a] It is a popular mechanism in the purchase of military equipment by governments. Offsets are also the basis of a number of local content regulations, such as the obligation in the conditions of a service contract to place a portion of contract value with domestic subcontractors; the licensing of technology to domestic manufacturers; and requirements for minimum inward investment by international equipment suppliers.

Use of offsets is explicitly excluded under Article XVI of the WTO Agreement on Government Procurement (GPA).[b] Exceptions are made for developing countries, which, at the time of accession, may negotiate conditions for their use. Under GPA rules, offsets—such as requirements for the incorporation of domestic content—are to be 'used only for qualification to participate in the procurement process and not as criteria for awarding contracts', and even within qualification processes, the request for offsets must be 'objective, clearly defined and non-discriminatory'.

Within tender documents, certain instructions to tenderers on local content could be considered offsets. These include:

- Preferential hiring and training of nationals
- Preferences for local sourcing
- Encouragement of inward investment
- Encouragement of support to domestic suppliers to develop future competitiveness
- Encouragement for operational infrastructure to be made available for public use; e.g. roads, power, water supply

A limiting factor in the use of offsets to drive local content (be that within government regulations or as a feature of the procurement strategy of a client oil, gas or mining company) is whether the costs involved for suppliers can be charged back to the client, and then whether the client can subsequently recover these costs against production revenues or tax. With regard to cost recovery, a dilemma arises if the economic benefits arising from the offsets are not able to be '*directly' related* to an approved work programme—this being the usual criterion for cost recovery eligibility.

a   J. Brauer and J. Dunne, *Arms Trade Offsets and Development* (Augusta, GA: College of Business Administration, 2005; carecon.org.uk/DPs/0504.pdf).
b   WTO, 'Uruguay Round Agreement, Agreement on Government Procurement, Article XVI'.

- Specific provisions relating to least-developed-country members, including flexibility to encourage foreign suppliers to assist in technology transfers and training through 'offsets', for example (see Box 1.4).[13]

## Agreement on Government Procurement

The plurilateral Agreement on Government Procurement (GPA) was negotiated in the Uruguay round and came into effect in 1996. These are rules for government procurement and apply only to those WTO members who are party to this particular agreement, in this case the countries of the European Union and 13 other countries, including Norway, USA, South Korea and Chinese Taipei.

The GPA rules are intended to counter internal political pressure to discriminate in favour of domestic suppliers of goods and services over foreign competitors, and thereby open up government-transacted business to international competition. A large part of the rules concern tendering procedures for contracts above specified financial thresholds, and include the following:[14]

- **Selective tendering**. Procedures for supplier selection (qualification of suppliers to tender and tendering processes) are not allowed to discriminate against foreign suppliers; for example, criteria for qualification and tendering must be limited to those essential to fulfil the contract, and not include offsets (see Box 1.4). Nor may technical specifications be used to discriminate against foreign suppliers, but should be based instead on international standards

- **Tender award**. Procuring entities are obliged to award contracts to the tenderer who has been determined to be fully capable of meeting the essential requirements of the contract; and either
  - is the lowest-priced tender, or

13 WTO, 'Uruguay Round Agreement, Agreement on Government Procurement, Article XVI'; www.wto.org/english/docs_e/legal_e/gpr-94_02_e.htm#ftnt7, 1996, accessed 9 June 2011.
14 *Ibid*.

  – the tender deemed to be the most advantageous in terms of a combination of evaluation criteria set forth in the tender documentation

- **Limited tendering**. Restricted tender lists (presumably including domestic-only tender lists and sole and single sourcing) is closely circumscribed, limited to: (i) situations of 'extreme urgency'; (ii) goods or components that are 'not interchangeable' with those from other suppliers; (iii) cases where extensions to construction contracts using a different service provider would be difficult for technical or economic reasons and cause 'significant inconvenience' (up to 50% of original contract value); and (iv) the award of contracts for repetition of 'similar' construction services, assuming that such a possibility was clearly indicated in the original notice to tenderers.

- **Rules of origin**. Parties to the GPA are not allowed to apply rules of origin to products or services which are different from the rules of origin applied in normal source of trade

In recognition of the economic development, financial and trade needs of poorer countries, the GPA carries time-limited exemptions for developing countries. Of the world's main oil and gas producers, those developing-country members and least developed countries that are members of the WTO are listed in Table 1.3.

The GPA has direct relevance to the oil and gas industry. Most critically, 'coverage' of the rules—meaning the types of public entity to which the rules apply—is determined by each member country, and can include state-owned entities and public utilities in the energy sector.

For example, South Korea includes the Korea National Oil Corporation in its list of entities obliged to procure in accordance with the GPA,[15] and Taiwan includes the Chinese Petroleum Corporation of Taiwan. This may partly explain the reluctance on the part of the Brazilian Government and other governments of oil and gas economies

15 WTO, 'Appendices and Annexes to the GPA', South Korea, Annex III of Appendix I; www.wto.org/english/tratop_e/gproc_e/appendices_e. htm#appendixI, accessed 9 June 2011.

to join the GPA, since presumably, unless able to negotiate exemptions, they would then be prohibited from requiring minimum levels of domestic content in the award of contracts.[16]

Table 1.3 **Oil- and gas-producing country members and observers of WTO**

| Developed-country WTO members | Developing-country WTO members | Least-developed-country WTO members | WTO observer status developing countries |
|---|---|---|---|
| • Switzerland | • UAE | • Angola | • Yemen |
| • Sweden | • Malaysia | • Chad | • Azerbaijan |
| • Singapore | • China | • Republic of Congo | • Russian Federation |
| • United States | • Brunei | | • Kazakhstan |
| • Germany | • Tunisia | | • Syria |
| • Japan | • Oman | | • Libya |
| • Finland | • Kuwait | | • Sudan |
| • Netherlands | • Thailand | | • Iraq |
| • Denmark | • Indonesia | | • Iran |
| • Canada | • India | | • Algeria |
| • Hong Kong SAR | • Brazil | | • Equatorial Guinea |
| • United Kingdom | • Vietnam | | • São Tomé & Principe |
| • Norway | • Turkey | | |
| • Australia | • Mexico | | |
| • Qatar | • Romania | | |
| • Saudi Arabia | • Colombia | | |
| • Italy | • Peru | | |
| | • Egypt | | |
| | • Trinidad and Tobago | | |
| | • Philippines | | |
| | • Argentina | | |
| | • Ecuador | | |
| | • Ghana | | |
| | • Venezuela | | |
| | • Nigeria | | |
| | • Gabon | | |

16 WTO, 'Trade Policy Review: Brazil', Record of Meeting, WT/TPR/M/212; www.wto.org/english/tratop_e/tpr_e/tp312_crc_e.htm, 2009, accessed 9 June 2011.

## Conclusions

This chapter has sought to demonstrate that it is not inevitable that local content regulations should lead to protectionism; nor is it so that they invariably lead to a more skilled, capable and competitive local industrial base, as governments may like to believe. The challenge facing those who formulate local content regulations is how to ensure expenditure in the oil, gas and mining sectors drives forward industrialisation of their country without trapping the local supplier industry in a cycle of protectionism.

The chapter has offered an important test of impending protectionism: namely, whether a local content regulation will break the core principle that, regardless of externalities and offsets, a contract should be awarded on the basis of international competitiveness in price, quality and delivery.

Three arguments have been forwarded to justify some limited protectionism for domestic suppliers in developing countries. However, an analysis of WTO rules suggests that under these agreements such arguments are acceptable only if time-limited, and that invariably procurement should in due course return to the core principle—the golden thread—of contract award on an internationally competitive basis.

# 2

# Local content optimisation

## Modelling the economic impact of local content on commercial interests and public industrial policy

### Local content as a strategic factor

In many emerging economies rich in mineral resources, local content is becoming a strategic consideration in investment decisions and project delivery. To illustrate, in Kazakhstan, legislation passed in 2010 mandates that new concession agreements to develop subsoil resources must deliver a minimum Kazakhstan content in personnel employed and in goods, works and services.[1] This law is being operationalised through a range of local content regulations. These include the setting of minimum local content targets in the award of major contracts; Kazakh-only tender lists for materials that Kazakh producers have a proven capability in supplying; and a minimum

---

1 Republic of Kazakhstan, Law of the Republic of Kazakhstan on Subsoil and Subsoil Use, 2010.

share of contract value to be awarded to Kazakh suppliers and sub-contractors within contracts won by international contractors.

Such regulations may well carry not only commercial implications for investors, operators, developers and service contractors, but also public policy implications: for example, if they lead to a reduction in national revenues or disincentive to inward investment. The challenge for investors and regulators is knowing which regulations will have precisely what degree of impact, and on whose strategic interests. Certain local content regulations, such as reporting requirements, may be fairly benign, while others may facilitate commercial or public policy objectives to be substantively modified.

Local content is also becoming a strategic consideration in project delivery. For example, in November 2010, Petrobras (the Brazilian national oil company) with its partners BG Group, Galp Energia, and Repsol, agreed contracts of US$3.46 billion with the Brazilian engineering contractor Engevix Engenharai S.A. in a strategic partnership with Swedish FPSO and platform builder GVA to construct a series of eight hulls for floating oil and gas production vessels.[2] The contract is a demonstration of the Brazilian Government delivering on its policy to increase local content and revitalise the Brazilian shipbuilding industry as an intended consequence of developing the hydrocarbons offshore in the Santos Basin.

The eight hulls are being built in the Rio Grande Naval Pole dry dock shipyard in the state of Rio Grande do Sul, with local content required to reach 70%. The yard is a wholly new facility. As such, construction work at the yard inevitably carries elevated risks to investors: first, in the form of potential cost escalation, when compared with the international shipbuilding markets of Singapore, South Korea and China; and, second, with the risk of delay to deployment of the vessels offshore, and the knock-on effect of this on investors' ability to meet commitments to shareholders on first-oil, the timing of production volumes and on investment returns.

In an effort to counter these risks, all eight hulls are to be new builds (rather than conversions from existing vessels), and will use standardised equipment and a repeatable, 'cookie-cutter' design. This

2  Subsea IQ; www.subseaiq.com/data/PrintProject.aspx?project_id=536&AspxAutoDetectCookieSupport=1, accessed 21 June 2011.

will arguably allow for economies of scale (such as the bulk purchase of steel), enable an accelerated learning curve for Brazilian workers and project managers, and ultimately bring costs down vessel by vessel until price parity with international markets is achieved.[3]

What the two examples above demonstrate is that in making investment decisions and in assuring that projects are delivered as anticipated, investors and national governments and their regulators may need to take early and strategic consideration of local content. This chapter considers three such strategic considerations, as follows:

- When negotiating new **concession agreements**,[4] what adjustments would be needed to accommodate mandatory targets on local content?

- How will new **local content regulations** and targets affect the commercial returns of investing companies?

- In the formulation of **contracting strategies** for major projects, what is the optimal level of local content that would satisfy both private and public interests?

Given the strategic importance of these questions, it is perhaps surprising that companies and regulators seem to undertake so little quantitative modelling to inform their decision-making around local content. There are at least four reasons that explain this omission:

First, investors and operating companies tend to direct their economic modelling internally at their own commercial interests, rather than explore how such interests might best be served by concurrently

---

3  A. Justi, F.P. Guedes, J.C.A. Filho, J.R.F. Almeida, M.R. Valle, R. Gonçalves, R. Moro, PETROBRAS, A.B.S. Almeida and ACCENTURE, *Pre-Salt: The Brazilian Opportunity to Take Local Industry to the Next Level* (Houston, TX: OTC, 2009).

4  In this chapter the term 'concession agreement' is used generically, defined here as any agreement made between a state and a company for the exploration or development of mining resources (metals, minerals, oil or gas) in which the state offers incentives, such as exclusivity to seek profit, reduced tax or royalty rates, cost recovery or production sharing arrangements, in exchange for long-term capital investment in the country.

aligning with the industrial and supply chain development policies of the host government.

Second, when local content regulations are perceived to challenge the commercial returns of investors, the response of investors is often framed by legal representation—a challenge to be addressed through dispensation clauses in concession agreements, joint operating agreements or tender procedures; or an issue to be resolved through arbitration. With legal teams steering such negotiations, the importance of precisely quantifying the potential erosion of commercial value may be overlooked.

Third, local content regulations are predominantly a political issue, viewed by policy-makers as a tool for delivering on public commitments to create jobs, support domestic suppliers or provide economic benefits to local populations. In this context, publicity for new local content regulations and tangible progress in reporting measurable increases in local content become the priority, while quantifying the relative impact of new regulations on investors and the potential for conflict with other public policy takes second place.

Fourth, it is possible that some policy-makers mistakenly believe local content to be a benign policy, with little consequential impact for other government priorities, specifically national competitiveness, government revenues, inward investment and anti-corruption. An absence of effort to quantify the unintended policy consequences of local content regulations may simply be a lack of awareness.

To address this need for better quantitative modelling of local content, and to answer the commercial and regulatory questions posed in this introduction, the remainder of the chapter applies an economic impact optimisation (EIO) model to quantify the impacts of different local content scenarios. The model has been developed by the firm Local Content Solutions for use in training and for customisation with oil, gas and mining clients.

# A hypothetical scenario

The model is applied to the hypothetical case of a new sub-surface natural resource development,[5] located onshore in a remote coastal region of an emerging economy. The volume of economically recoverable minerals is already known and, once the concession agreement is finalised, the development company, on behalf of its investors (which includes a 20% stake by a state-owned company), can proceed to project execution.

Road and rail links to the concession area are good, and there are two towns, one 10 km away with 50,000 inhabitants, the other 30 km away with 300,000; the latter is located on the coast with mature port facilities.

The concession agreement being negotiated is the second such concession granted in the region. As such there is an established local supplier industry in both towns, with ten years' experience in providing goods and services to a similar-sized and similarly configured operation, but one that is now past its peak production.

The project concept involves US$6 billion capital investment over five years, comprising in-house engineering design, sub-surface engineering works, on-site power generation and processing facilities, and with evacuation via an upgraded road infrastructure to the local port. The operational life of the field is 24 years. The main modules and assumptions of the EIO model applied to this scenario are summarised in Box 2.1.

---

5 The case is intentionally non-specific about the type of mining involved, so as to be of relevance to readers from both the mineral/metals and hydrocarbon sectors.

## Box 2.1 **Modules and assumptions of the EIO model**

This chapter uses an Excel-based economic impact optimisation (EIO) model to assess the commercial and public policy implications of different regulations and strategies for local content and supplier development. The four modules and core assumptions of the model are as follows:

**Modules:**

- **Economic environment module**. Inflation rate, sales price, royalty and tax rates, government equity share, volume of recoverable minerals, rate of capital expenditure recovery/depreciation, production revenue sharing rates (sliding scale)
- **Costs and procurement module**. Capital expenditure, operational expenditure, spread of expenditure across procurement categories
- **Local content scenario module**. Maximum local content if contracts awarded on internationally competitive basis; maximum local content with premiums for additional training and management supervision; maximum local content with capital investment, including associated schedule delays
- **Results module**
    - Impact on local content
    - Impact on costs
    - Impact on schedule
    - NPV (net present value) and IRR (internal rate of return)
    - Payback period
    - National revenues and taxes
    - Jobs created (direct, indirect, induced)
    - Investments in local supplier competitiveness

**Core assumptions:**

- Local content defined as proportion of contract value spent on goods and services of domestic origin
- Expenditure aggregated by contract type
- Cost of premiums to increase local content proportionate to local content achieved. Rates differ for training and supervision vs. capital investment
- Training and supervision premiums spread across capital and operational expenditure. Capital investment premiums all in year one of capital expenditure
- Capital investments to build local capability charged to investors at 50% of total cost (remainder taken by government, first-tier contractors or finance institution)
- Schedule delays defer start date for investment, but construction period and IRR remain unchanged

# Negotiating concession terms to deliver local content targets

Taking the first of our strategic considerations—'when negotiating new concession agreements, what adjustments would be needed to accommodate mandatory targets on local content?'—let us assume that the regulatory authorities recently introduced a new law on sub-soil mining (hydrocarbons, minerals and metals), and that this law requires capital expenditure to achieve 40% local content and operational expenditure 60%. The new law is applicable to the current concession negotiations.

To inform these negotiations the investing consortium carried out a local market survey and concluded that, for their base-case project concept, domestic supplier capacity could support 20% local content in capital expenditure and 36% in operations.

Framed by the terms of the adjacent mining concession, the government and investing consortium have entered these negotiations with the following assumed terms:

- No signatory payment

- 25% royalty payment on gross sales

- 70% maximum annual recovery of capital expenditure on net revenues after royalties

- Sharing of production revenues (after royalties and cost recovery) of 30:70 state: investors up to 40,000 units production per day, and 60:40 for higher volumes thereafter[6]

- A composite tax rate (corporation tax, import duties, withholding taxes, and regional and local taxes) of 30%[7]

---

6 Many concession contracts, especially in mining for metals and minerals, depend on the tax regime to apportion state vs. investor revenues, rather than production sharing. The EIO model accommodates both types of arrangement.

7 Clearly this is a generalised tax figure for illustrative purposes. In reality rates will differ.

The introduction of mandatory local content minimum targets into the negotiations was news to the investors who had assumed that, as per the previous concession, domestic suppliers would be preferenced only if internationally competitive on price, quality, volumes and delivery; that is, 20% and 36% local content for capital and operational expenditure, respectively.

Based on these initial, pre-law assumptions, and a production period of 24 years, the projected rate of return (IRR) for the investing consortium was 12.0% (US$0.8 billion at a 10% discount rate). The investors had set themselves an IRR threshold for investment of 10%, below which the investment committee would reject the proposal. Applying the EIO model to these parameters, at the new mandated 40% and 60% targets for local content, the 10% minimum threshold for investment returns is breached, with the IRR falling to 9.3% and NPV turning negative by US$0.4 billion (refer to Table 2.1).

Table 2.1 **Modelled impact of mandated local content targets on NPV and IRR**

| Local content scenario | % Local content in CAPEX | % Local content in OPEX | NPV (10% discount rate) | IRR (%) |
|---|---|---|---|---|
| Base case | 20 | 36 | US$0.8 billion | 12.0 |
| New regulations | 40 | 60 | US$0.4 billion | 9.3 |

CAPEX, capital expenditure; OPEX, operational expenditure

The EIO model was then used to spread the gross local content target of 40% across the different expenditure categories. This meant assuming higher than 40% for sub-categories of expenditure where the cost of achieving local content was proportionately less than for other categories; for example module fabrication versus long-lead equipment.

The EIO model suggests that achieving 40% local content would require additional cost premiums of US$1.4 billion for investment in training, new equipment and plant. US$270 million of these premiums would be required to raise local content in domestic module fabrication capabilities from 12%, on the basis of an internationally competitive tender, to 27%. After ten years, although the local region supports some fabrication services, there is no capability to assemble the complex equipment integral to the scope of work. The 12% local content that the investors' market surveys showed was possible mainly comprises fabrication services to complete and then install the modules. To reach 27% would require a wholly new level of inward investment in finishing and assembly capability, involving international manufacturers in a suite of alliances with local fabricators and manufacturers, as well as capital investment to construct larger and more sophisticated fabrication facilities. Such capital investments, even if shared with government and finance institutions, would escalate the overall costs of the project, and delay the start of the construction phase by approximately 12 months.

Figure 2.1 shows the aggregate level of additional cost premiums required to reach the new targets of 40% and 60% local content in capital and operational expenditure, respectively.

Figure 2.1 **Impact of new local content regulations on project and operational costs**

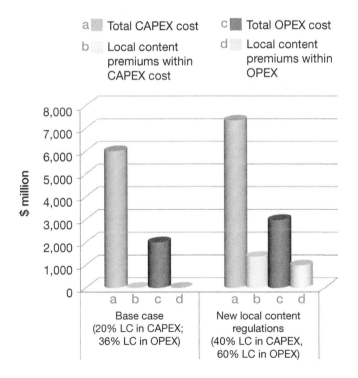

The size of these premiums and their adverse impact on investment returns suggest that either the local content targets be reduced,
or the other terms of the concession are renegotiated (perhaps not
impossible if you recall that the state has a 20% interest in the venture). Table 2.2 shows how each parameter, taken in isolation, would
have to change in order to achieve both the new local content targets
and sustain the base-case IRR of 12%. In summary, either royalties
would need to fall from 25% to 5%, or production sharing, when in
the higher-volume band, would need to be reversed from 60:40 in
favour of the state, to 60:40 in favour of the investors.

In this scenario, the EIO modelling suggests that other parameters
are less sensitive. Thus, moving from 70% to 100% allowable cost
recovery against net revenues would improve the IRR by an insufficient 0.2%; likewise, reducing tax rates to zero would improve IRR
by 0.7%.

The final row of Table 2.2 provides a possible composite set of
adjusted terms, designed to deliver, concurrently, a 12% IRR and the
new mandated local content targets.

Table 2.2 **Adjustments to proposed concession terms to meet
local content targets and maintain 12% IRR**

| Local content | Royalty rate | Cost recovery rate | Production sharing split | Composite tax rate |
| --- | --- | --- | --- | --- |
| Base case 21% CAPEX 36% OPEX | 25% | 70% | 30:70 60:40 | 30% |
| Parameters in isolation 40% CAPEX 60% OPEX | 5% | 100% insufficient | 30:70 40:60 | 0% insufficient |
| Composite parameters 40% CAPEX 60% OPEX | 19% | 80% | 30:70 50:50 | 25% |

If, however, the investing consortium were willing to accept their
minimum IRR of 10%, and assuming the government was unwilling

to compromise on royalty payments, cost recovery or the tax regime, then a 10% net change in the sharing of net production revenues in the higher band (from 60:40 to 55:45) would be sufficient to support the additional premiums needed to deliver the mandated local content targets.

Whether in reality such negotiations would lead to compromise on the core terms of concession agreements is debatable. But, even if not, modelling the impact of local content on future investment costs and returns, and showing how concession terms would need to respond to retain the same margins, would provide a readily comprehensible measure of the strategic importance of local content in such discussions.

## Quantifying the commercial impact of different local content regulations

Let us now move on in time and assume that the said law was not in place when the concession agreement was signed, but that the base case described in the previous section prevailed; that is, local content is driven by the principle of contract award on an internationally competitive basis and is likely to be 20% for capital expenditure and 36% for operations. Let us also assume that the terms of the concession remained as per the adjacent concession: namely, royalties 25%, cost recovery 70%, sharing of net revenues 30:70/60:40, and a tax rate of 30%.

Under this new scenario, the US$6 billion development project has been sanctioned by the authorities and investing consortium, and a development company established to deliver the project. The company is at the pre-FEED (front-end engineering and design) stage of project engineering, having adopted a preferred base-case concept and detailed cost estimates categorised according to a provisional contracting strategy. We will assume that at this stage the policy imperative for increased local content had not been factored into the original negotiation of the concession agreement (there were no minimum targets set at this time), nor considered material to the selection of the preferred project concept.

Now let us introduce the newly formed Local Content Development Authority (LCDA)—part of the Ministry for Minerals and Energy. The LCDA has just issued a suite of draft local content regulations for consultation. The development company and its investors have been asked to consider these regulations. The proposed regulations are as follows:

- A 15% nominal price advantage at tender stage for nationally registered service providers and suppliers who provide goods and services of 'domestic origin'[8]

- Domestic-only tender lists for the procurement of materials and provision of services for which the respective industry association considers that domestic suppliers have the necessary 'capability'

- For contracts won by international contractors, a minimum of 40% of the contract value to be channelled to domestic subcontractors and suppliers

Application of the EIO model allows the impact of these different regulations to be compared. Table 2.3 captures the estimated level of local content that each regulation would introduce to the six main categories of the provisional contracting strategy. In the table, the base case represents the maximum level of local content achievable within each category if contracts are awarded on an internationally competitive basis for price, delivery and quality.

In applying the EIO model, the following assumptions have been made:

- The **15% nominal price advantage** on contract award is applicable only to expenditure where domestic suppliers and contractors would successfully pass pre-qualification processes and the minimum mandatory thresholds within the technical part of an invitation to tender. The regulation also only applies to first-tier contractors; that is, the rule does

8 For the purposes of this chapter we will assume that 'domestic origin' is where 50% of the sales price of goods or services stays within the domestic economy; that is, it does not go to pay for the import of components, equipment or materials, or to expat or overseas-based labour.

Table 2.3 **Impact of new local content regulations on contracting categories**

| Proposed local content regulations | Contracting categories (% local content) | | | | | | |
| --- | --- | --- | --- | --- | --- | --- | --- |
| | Project manage-ment and pre-FEED (in-house) | Long lead times | EPCm module fabrication | EPC con-struction and instal-lation | EPIC sub-surface engineering | Directly contracted services | Direct purchase/ lease of equipment and materials |
| Base case (no change to LC regulations) | 11% | 2% | 12% | 30% | 5% | 60% | 35% |
| 15% price nominal advantage for domestic suppliers | 11% | 2% | 13% | 33% | 5% | 70% | 37% |
| Domestic-only tender lists where 'capable' | 11% | 2% | 14% | 35% | 5% | 75% | 48% |
| 40% contract value to domestic suppliers in international contracts | 11% | 15% max | 40% | 40% | 15% max | 76% | 60% max |

EPCm, engineering, procurement and construction-management; EPC, engineering, procurement and construction; EPIC, engineering, procurement, installation and commissioning

not flow down to tendering processes for subcontracts. It is assumed that this rule leads to an average 10% actual price escalation for applicable contracts

- Regarding **domestic-only tender lists**, the industry associations in the country apply a fairly loose definition of 'capability', assuming that if any domestic supplier or service provider has previously provided the relevant good or service under contract, then de facto they would be internationally competitive and eligible to be put on a domestic-only tender list. This is so, regardless of the developer's specific requirements on quality, volume and international benchmarked pricing. The regulation is applicable to both directly and indirectly procured services and goods, and would include such services as security, scaffolding, office maintenance and vehicle maintenance, and the supply of materials such as piping, bolts, gaskets, cables, certain valves and concrete. The rule does not envisage a relaxation of minimum technical requirements, but given the considerable 'stretch' required of many of these local firms to meet specifications, it is anticipated that premiums would be needed in additional on-the-job training and management supervision, and in some cases upfront capital investment, to ensure that volumes and delivery schedules can be met

- The rule on a **minimum 40% local content** within international contracts is intended to incentivise partnerships and consortium bidding among international and domestic firms, leading to inward investment and technology transfer. These alliances can be either joint ventures or arrangements whereby the international firm nominates domestic subcontractors and suppliers as part of its tender

Based on these assumptions, and taken in isolation, the 15% price advantage rule drives overall local content in capital expenditure up 1.9%, at a cost of US$110 million in premiums for additional training and supervision. The introduction of domestic-only tender lists for directly contracted services and materials raises local content by 3.6%, requires US$230 million in premiums (US$140 million for on-the-job training, management supervision and quality controls, and US$89 million in capital investments), and introduces a 12 month delay to allow local suppliers of materials to develop greater volume capacity.

Taken in isolation, most impactful is the proposed rule for a minimum of 40% local content within international contracts. This drives local content up 16 percentage points to 36% of capital expenditure. However, to achieve this requires premiums of US$990 million and an 18 month delay to the start of construction, owing to the need for new capital investment in new manufacturing capability and module fabrication facilities.

Looking in more detail, informed by market surveys, the development company established that the maximum achievable local content in international contracts for the long-lead items (compressors, instrumentation, etc.), sub-surface engineering and the direct purchasing or leased equipment and material is 15%, 15% and 60%, respectively. To achieve these maximums requires an increase in project costs of US$480 million over 18 months, essentially to build in-country equipment repair and maintenance service capability and capacity.

The impact of the regulations on capital expenditure has been described above. Figures 2.2 and 2.3 show how these different local content regulations play out against the wider commercial and public policy objectives of the investors and government, taking into consideration both capital and operational expenditure over the life of the project. In particular, the figures provide insight into the trade-offs between the impact on job creation (direct, indirect and induced) and cost premiums, and between government revenues and local content.

Figure 2.4 plots the local content achieved for the proposed regulations, and their impact on the internal rate of return for the investing consortium.

Owing to the cost premiums required to meet these new regulations, all four proposals erode investment returns to below the 12% IRR base case. The greatest impact on IRR is the 40% minimum local content in international contracts. As the project is currently configured, this regulation alone causes the project to fail to achieve the minimum acceptable IRR for investment of 10%.

In other words, even in isolation, the 40% minimum local content proposal is an investment 'show stopper', primarily because the only means to achieve this is to allow for substantial capital investment in manufacturing, assembly and module fabrication capability.

Figure 2.2 **Impact of local content regulations on jobs and cost premiums**

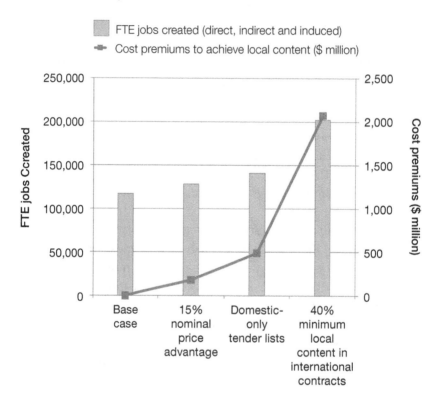

FTE, full-time equivalent

Figure 2.3 **Impact of local content regulations on government revenues**

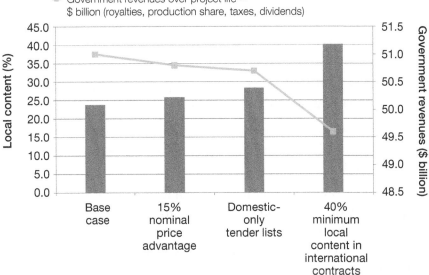

Figure 2.4 **Impact of local content regulations on investment returns (IRR)**

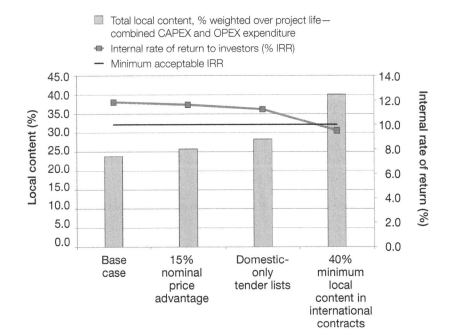

# Quantifying local content within contracting strategies

In this last modelling scenario we will assume that two of the four proposed new regulations on local content have become mandatory, namely:

- A 15% nominal price advantage to producers and suppliers of services and goods of domestic origin

- Domestic-only tender lists for materials and services where local suppliers are deemed 'capable' by representative industry bodies

The pre-FEED engineering is now complete, and the procurement department of the development company is about to convene a workshop where different contracting strategies will be compared for their impact on cost, risk (interface, schedule, quality, asset integrity) and local content. At the workshop, the three considerations relating to local content will be: (i) Do the contracting strategies comply with the new regulations? (ii) What costs will be incurred in order to comply; and (iii) How will these costs impact on investment returns?

Two contracting strategies are under consideration, as follows:

- **Stick-build strategy.** The main construction and fabrication work is carried out near the project site, and the scope of work is unbundling to maximise access to procurement opportunities for local construction services contractors

- **Modular strategy.** The project components are pre-assembled in fabrication yards both in-country located along the coast (to spread the economic benefits) and overseas, and then transported to the site through the nearby port and upgraded road infrastructure

Figures 2.5 and 2.6 contrast the two (much simplified) contracting strategies.

Figure 2.5 **'Stick-build' contracting strategy**

| Scope Component | Project management | Engineering | Procurement | Construction | Commissioning |
|---|---|---|---|---|---|
| Port and road upgrades | PM | E&P | | Construction | |
| Labour camp and utilities | | | | | |
| Site preparation | | | | | |
| Power supply unit | EPCm | | | Construction | |
| Sub-surface excavation | EPIC | | | | |
| Processing facilities | EPCm | | | Construction | |

Figure 2.6 **'Modular' contracting strategy**

| Scope Component | Project management | Engineering | Procurement | Construction | Commissioning |
|---|---|---|---|---|---|
| Port and road upgrades | EPC | | | Construction | |
| Labour camp and utilities | | | | | |
| Site preparation | | | | | |
| Power supply unit | EPIC | | | | |
| Sub-surface excavation | EPIC | | | | |
| Processing facilities | EPIC | | | | |

## Analysis of the 'stick-build' contracting strategy

Application of the EIO model demonstrates that the 'stick-build' contracting strategy can be configured to meet the new local content compliance requirements. For example, unbundling the various civil and facilities construction contracts fosters compliance with providing opportunities for 'capable' local service providers pursuant to the new regulation for domestic-only tender lists.

This contracting strategy can also support elevated levels of local content in directly contracted construction minor services of up to 80%. However, the EIO model anticipates schedule risks in delivering such high levels of content, and calculates that managing these risks would demand a cost premium of US$36 million to strengthen the capacity and capabilities of these local contractors. This is not investment that can take place on the job, but requires upfront capital investment and would subsequently delay the start of the project by eight months.

The 15% price advantage for domestic suppliers of directly procured equipment and materials would result in local content of 51% but, likewise, to assure quality, volumes and delivery, premiums of US$77 million would be needed to develop production capability, adding a further four month delay.

From a government policy perspective, the 'stick-build' contracting strategy would deliver a weighted overall average of 27.5% local content, generate 82,350 jobs during construction (although many of these would be temporary and include induced employment) and bring US$480 million of new investment into the domestic industrial base, of which US$113 million is long-term capital investment.

## Analysis of the modular contracting strategy

In comparison, the 'modular' contracting strategy supports a series of autonomous lump-sum EPIC contracts for the construction of power supply unit, the sub-surface excavation work and processing facilities. The strategy also includes a single EPC contract, combining all civil and related works (with the exception of a single, directly contracted construction contract to embrace the new regulation on domestic-only tender lists).

This contracting strategy has certain advantages for project delivery. It reduces the number of management interfaces, and puts downward pressure on cost and risk by enabling international specialist contractors to manage all aspects of the scope of work and utilise their established global framework agreements to source equipment, materials and labour.

From the developer and investors' perspective, the strategy is commercially advantageous; however, it fails to comply with the local content regulations. From a government policy perspective, the 'cradle-to-grave' nature of these international contracts effectively locks out purportedly capable domestic suppliers and service providers.

In summary, the modular contracting strategy supports up to 20.8% local content compared with 27.5% for the 'stick-build' option, generates 19,950 fewer jobs, and brings US$67 million of new investment into the local industry. Most of this investment is in the form of additional on-the-job training, management supervision and quality control to support the modular fabrication work being carried out in-country. Table 2.4 contrasts the two contracting strategies.

Table 2.4 **Comparison of contracting strategies**

| Stick-build | Modular |
| --- | --- |
| 27.5 % local content | 20.8% local content |
| Local content compliance | Local content non-compliance |
| 82,350 FTE jobs | 62,400 FTE jobs |
| US$480 million capital investment in local industry | US$67 million investment in on-the-job training and supervision of local suppliers |
| Stick-build carries a 7.8% cost variance with modular | |

Figure 2.7 further contrasts the two contracting strategies in terms of their contribution to total national income: that is, the combination of royalty receipts, state share of production revenues, corporate and other taxes, and dividends (the latter being the assumed share of post-tax profit taken by the 20% state interest in the venture).

Figure 2.7 **Comparison of national revenues under stick-build versus modular contracting strategy**

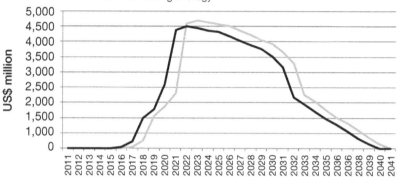

It can be seen that peak revenues for the stick-build strategy accrue a year behind the modular strategy, but are US$200 million higher, while cumulative national income over the life of the project is US$52.7 billion for the stick-build strategy and US$50.8 billion for the modular, a difference of US$1.9 billion.

# Some limitations of local content optimisation modelling

Clearly, the quantifications presented in this chapter are only as accurate as the quality of the model, the data being used and the assumptions made. In practice, the EIO model applied here would be customised and calibrated to the strategic alternatives under consideration, the local supplier market and the commercial interests and public policy priorities that the particular situation presents.

In this chapter, I hope to have demonstrated the power of even a simplified model such as this to inform dialogue between oil, gas and mining companies and investors on the one hand, and government regulators and ministries on the other, about where the trade-offs and opportunities lie when striving for higher levels of local content.

At present, it is quite possible that new local content laws and regulations are being introduced without sufficient quantitative analysis of whether they may conflict with other public policies: for example, the attraction of inward investment, development of industrial competitiveness, or raising and timing of national revenues.

Likewise, senior managers in oil, gas and mining companies sometimes react against new local content regulations or internal 'do good' pressure for higher levels of local content, without first precisely quantifying what these objections are.

If all stakeholders were to have a more quantified understanding of the commercial and public policy impacts of local content and associated regulations and strategies, it may well be that sensible, optimal regulatory and engineering solutions could be realised—solutions that support industrial development and reliable and cost-efficient project delivery, without destroying investment returns or conflicting with other public policies.

## Applications of EIO modelling

Below is a list of the potential applications of EIO modelling to support the management of local content as a strategic issue.

1. **Concession negotiations**. The strategic consequences of local content targets, negotiated as part of concession agreements

2. **New local content regulations**. How proposals for driving local content and supplier development through new laws, regulations, tender procedures and so on impact on commercial interests and public industrial policy

3. **Investment decisions**. How different project concepts and engineering options compare in terms of their potential for local content and supplier development, and the impact of this on commercial interests and public policy

4. **Contracting strategy**. The impact of different contracting and procurement strategies on meeting local content regulations and on commercial interests and public industrial policy

5. **ESIA (environmental and social impact assessment studies)**. Strengthening economic analysis within ESIA studies to identify optimal measures to enhance the socioeconomic impacts of major projects (jobs and supplier development) without damaging commercial interests. At present ESIA provides only a static assessment of positive socioeconomic impacts

6. **Company local content strategy**. Many companies now prepare and update dedicated local content strategy documents for each of the country businesses units. These strategies need to be assessed for their impacts on commercial interests and alignment with public industrial policy

7. **Government industrial policy options**. Assessment of different policy options, leading to a clear understanding of their limits to avoid harming the investment climate or fuelling protectionism

## Conclusions

This chapter has demonstrated the utility of economic impact optimisation modelling as a tool for investors and developers to run scenarios based on the local content requirements of a particular country, and for government policy-makers and informers to gauge the consequences of local content laws and regulations. But, as with all such tools, it is all about timing. Will it be possible to apply EIO modelling with a country's politicians and public servants before they pass legislation, or before they lock themselves into the public pronouncements of new local content regulations and targets? And will developers apply such modelling early enough to inform their assessment of project alternatives and contracting strategies?

# 3
# Procurement strategy
## The role of contracting and procurement strategy in effective local content management

One definition of 'procurement' is a process that seeks to secure equipment, materials and services at the *right price*, at the *right time*, to the *right quality*, in the *right quantity* and from the *right place*.[1] These five 'rights' are not mutually exclusive, and can result in pressure to make trade-offs. It is the necessity to minimise these trade-offs that means that clients need to be strategic in their procurement planning for a particular investment, project or operation.

For example, if the key business objective of a client for a capital project is the earliest possible commissioning date, and the proposed design has been proven but only in locations outside of the host country, then the client may elect to use a procurement strategy that tenders the bulk of the design, purchase of goods and construction

1 Adapted from: S. Emmett and B. Crocker, *Excellence in Procurement: How to Optimise Costs and Add Value* (Cambridge, UK: Cambridge Academic, 2008).

services on the basis of a fixed-price, turnkey contract, with a tender list comprising experienced international lead contractors.

Such a strategy makes commercial sense with regard to the all-important schedule ('right time'), and is likely to also deliver on the right quantities and quality. If progressed as a contested tender with 'lowest price wins', then the same strategy would also foster the right price. But what of 'place'?

Major international contractors frequently have long-term global sourcing arrangements with key equipment and material suppliers, enabling them to drive down costs and achieve a competitive edge. However, these deals may crowd out domestic suppliers, even if these suppliers are capable and potentially competitive in their own right. Thus, if we equate 'right place' to mean delivering local content within a project's total expenditure (for example, as measured by the % of total spend on goods and services of domestic origin), then under a procurement strategy driven by schedule we may find that local content (place) is traded off against schedule (time). This trade-off is illustrated in Figure 3.1.

Figure 3.1 **Schematic of the trade-off between local content and schedule**

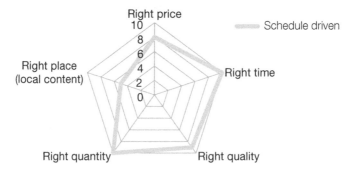

But what happens if delivering local content is a legal requirement or strong commercial imperative: for example, in a scenario where the recovery of expenditure costs is compromised if local content compliance targets are not met in full. At the same time, let us factor in the not uncommon practice of regulators setting local content percentage targets at levels higher than the capability of the domestic supplier market to supply goods and services on an internationally competitive basis. A procurement strategy that facilitates compliance with these local content targets (i.e. gives uncompetitive preference to domestic suppliers) will probably have an impact on both project price and schedule, and possibly also quality and quantity. In Figure 3.2 the implications of this type of percentage local content-driven procurement strategy on the five 'rights' is contrasted with a schedule-driven strategy.

Figure 3.2 **Schematic comparison of procurement strategies: schedule driven versus % local content driven**

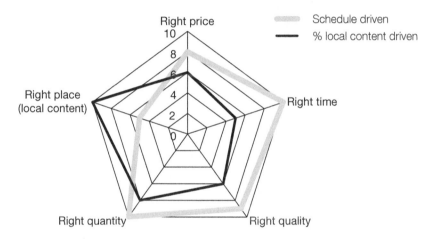

Figure 3.3 takes the illustration a step further. Here we introduce a scenario where the client is not compelled to meet local content percentage targets. Instead, for reasons of corporate reputation and long-term cost efficiencies, a procurement strategy is adopted that encourages international contractors to partner with, or subcontract to, domestic suppliers in ways that develop their skill, technical capability and competitiveness (i.e. their ability to meet schedules, avoid cost escalation, deliver on quality and quantity, and be more competitive in the future).

Figure 3.3 **Schematic comparison of procurement strategies: % local content driven versus local supplier development driven, against base of schedule driven**

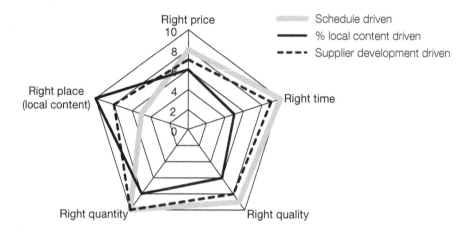

Overall, the negative impact of this supplier development-driven procurement strategy on the other four 'rights' is less pronounced than with the percentage local content-driven strategy. Note, however, that 'price' is still assumed to include a small premium to support technology transfer from international to domestic firms, offset price distortions (such as the higher logistic costs of importing components for domestic assembly), or cover the increased liabilities and risk faced by the international contractor. We assume that this premium is less than the cost implication of complying with excessive local content percentage targets. Further, under this strategy the overall proportion of local content within expenditure will be less than in the target-driven strategy, since international contractors are taking more of the procurement budget.

Of course, formulating a procurement strategy is more complex than in this scenario. In practice there are multiple business objectives to consider, and a variety of commercial and non-commercial risks. Procurement strategies for large projects (referred to as contracting strategies) have to consider whether to integrate the procurement of different categories of expenditure (design, project management, equipment and materials, construction services, production and operations management, distribution, etc.), as well as whether to contract together or keep separate the procurement of different project components (e.g. production units, utilities, civil works, transportation). Such complexity requires a patchwork of interlocking procurement sub-strategies.

Effective consideration of local content within the formulation of procurement strategies is essentially a three-step process. First, it is about understanding what level of priority the business should give to local content when compared with the other four 'rights' of price, time, quality and schedule, and what value creation or protection might be anticipated from formulating a strategy that enhances local content.

Second, it is about understanding the local supplier market. This means quantifying the client's forward demand for goods and services, and reconciling this with the capabilities, capacity and competitiveness of local and national suppliers to meet this demand. Third, it is about formulating tailored, procurement-driven solutions, which include the packaging of work, deciding on the extent of client control over contracts and contract interfaces and designing compensation arrangements. The remainder of this chapter describes these three steps in turn

# Prioritising local content within procurement strategy

Key drivers for local content management in oil and gas development projects are given in Table 3.1. In formulating procurement strategy, it is crucial to know how important local content considerations are in relation to other factors that might influence the *same* value drivers. For example, with regard to reputation and alignment with host government economic priorities, how important is it to formulate a procurement strategy that delivers high levels of local content, compared with one that meets the government's anticipated schedule for production volumes or revenue raising. Or, with regard to managing commercial risks, what level of risk to overall project cost and schedule is posed by sourcing materials from higher-unit-priced, less experienced, local suppliers, compared with the higher freight and insurance costs and longer delivery times of importing the same materials from international suppliers.

Table 3.1 **Value drivers for local content management in the formulation of procurement strategy: upstream oil and gas development**

| Category | Value driver |
|---|---|
| Commercial risk | Manage risk that regulatory requirements or political pressure to utilise domestic suppliers will lead to higher award costs, cost escalation or schedule delays that then undermine investment returns |
| Compliance | Avoid fines and protect company reputation by meeting regulatory requirements for local content |
| Reputation | Build reputation and market differentiation with host government through innovation and economic impact in employment and training of nationals, local sourcing and domestic supplier development |
| Cost efficiency | Reduce costs by preferencing domestic suppliers or developing their capability. Cost savings may include: import duties, labour costs, logistics costs, total life costs of equipment due to localised repair and maintenance |
| Supply bottlenecks | Promote domestic supplier development as a strategy to address scarcity in global supplier chains |
| Cost recovery | Assure the recovery of investment costs in cases where (because of regulatory requirements, joint operating agreements or political pressures) recovery of these costs is tied to preferencing certain suppliers, meeting local content targets or developing supplier capability |
| Budget and permitting approvals | Use procurement to deliver local content closely aligned with government industrial priorities, thus preventing delays to budget approvals, permits and contract awards |

| Category | Value driver |
|---|---|
| Social licence to operate | Use local supply chain expenditure to provide economic opportunities for project-affected local communities and community-based suppliers, as part of compensation for disturbance, e.g. facilities maintenance contracts, agricultural supply agreements |
| Concession negotiations | Align project options and high-level procurement strategy with government industrial development priorities as a means to gain competitive advantage when bidding or negotiating new concession agreements |

# Understanding local supplier markets

Too many procurement strategies are prepared with insufficient information about the capability of the domestic supplier market. It is critical to have accurate information about where local suppliers benchmark on price, schedule and quality against competition from both within the domestic market and against international suppliers.

It is not sufficient to know whether a local trade association reports that there is 'some' capability in the country. Further information is needed about the *range* of products or services available, labour productivity, production *capacity* (e.g. the size of the fabrication yard, or throughput volumes of a particular product or service), the supplier's *experience* in providing similar products or services (including that of its senior managers), and its ability to *deliver* on time, at internationally competitive prices, with the right after-sales service and *maintenance*, to the right standards of *quality*, and with acceptable levels of *health, safety and environmental* performance.

To some extent, if the client keeps records, the past performance of suppliers will answer some of these questions. But for greenfield developments, or for new entrants in the local supplier market, or for periodic projects with significant time lags in between, such information will need to be sought proactively, in advance of formulating the procurement strategy.

In such cases, preliminary pre-qualification processes or selective local market benchmarking and market surveys will need to be targeted at the expenditure categories most relevant to the core value drivers for local content (refer to Table 3.1).

A key consideration in this type of market analysis will be how to classify different categories of expenditure against the capabilities of the domestic supplier market. Drawing on the work of Peter Kraljic[2] on purchasing strategy, one approach is to assess the level of risk arising from different suppliers. On this basis, suggested classifications are as follows:

- Categories of expenditure that if sourced locally would carry the **highest risks** to project or operational objectives, i.e. the cost, schedule or quality of a project would be materially compromised

- Categories of negligible or **low risk**, i.e. domestic suppliers can provide the goods and services on a routine and internationally competitive basis

- Categories where domestic suppliers carry **some risks**, but for which there is an imperative to procure locally, and thus ways must to be found to overcome these risks. Circumstances might include:
  - Where the client is being **compelled to source locally** because of either regulatory requirements (e.g. local content targets directed at certain spend categories), or political pressure to use certain nominated or state-owned companies
  - **Equipment and technology** categories of priority to the host government's industrial development, manufacturing or export policies
  - **Subcontractor services** where local employment and hiring opportunities are most likely to arise

2 P. Kraljic, 'Purchasing Must Become Supply Management', *Harvard Business Review* 61 (September–October 1983): 109-17.

– Categories that may encounter potential **local bottle-necks**, e.g. a shortage of certain skilled labour

A second consideration is to map the local supplier market onto the different outcomes for local content. There are broadly two types of outcome:

- **Type I: maximum proportion of local content within expenditure** (national workers or suppliers). This is applicable to categories of expenditure which, if sourced locally, either (i) carry low levels of risk, e.g. suppliers of *routine* materials and services; or (ii) carry some constraints or risks (such as gaps in certain skilled labour or plant capacity), but which if overcome would contribute significantly to the percentage of local content achieved across the operation or project, and therefore the client has an *appetite* to take on the risk or pay for the cost of risk mitigation

- **Type II: local skills and supplier competitiveness developed as part of contract execution**. Applicable to expenditure that (i) offers the client *leverage* to build the broad competences of national employees and/or strengthen the capabilities, capacity and future competitiveness of local suppliers (into this group would fall expenditure involving long-term contracts or a series of shorter-term contracts with replicable engineering or product specifications); or (ii) is critical to the operation or project and thus ways must be found to manage the commercial risks of sourcing these goods or services locally, e.g. lack of experienced project management, safety equipment, high-specification OEM (original equipment manufacturer) goods (compressors, turbines, heat exchangers)

Figure 3.4 is a version of the Kraljic expenditure classification matrix sometimes used to inform procurement strategy. The matrix has been adapted to identify four different categories of expenditure matched to the levels of risk posed by local suppliers and the type of local content management opportunity presented.

Figure 3.4 **Expenditure classification for local sourcing**

Source: Adapted from Kraljic

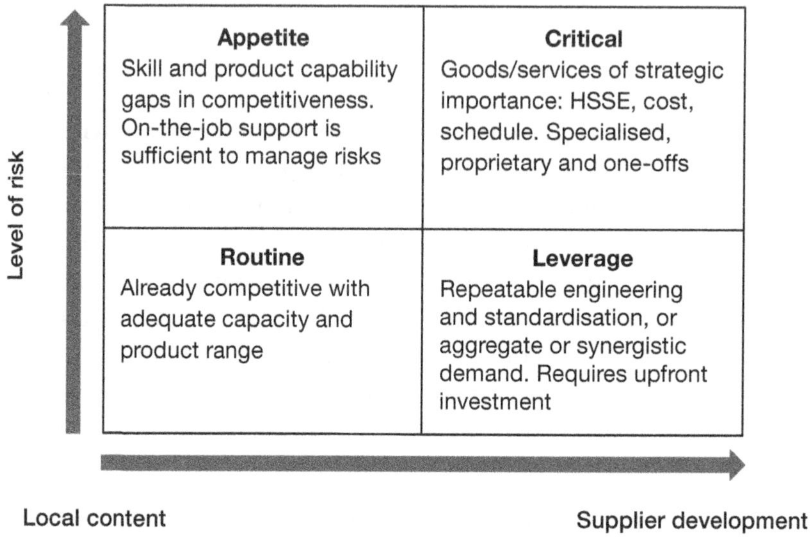

| | **Appetite** Skill and product capability gaps in competitiveness. On-the-job support is sufficient to manage risks | **Critical** Goods/services of strategic importance: HSSE, cost, schedule. Specialised, proprietary and one-offs |
|---|---|---|
| **Level of risk** | **Routine** Already competitive with adequate capacity and product range | **Leverage** Repeatable engineering and standardisation, or aggregate or synergistic demand. Requires upfront investment |

Local content                                    Supplier development

Linking local supplier market analysis to the formulation of procurement strategy in this way has similarities to recent events in Brazil, in the context of developing the offshore oil fields of the Santos Basin (see Box 3.1).

## Box 3.1 **Local supplier analysis and procurement strategy**

**Santos Basin Developments, Brazil**[a]

PROMINP is a joint initiative of the national Brazilian oil company Petrobras and Ministry of Mines and Energy. The organisation has identified aggregate demand for oil and gas development in the Santos Basin over the next 20 years and compared this with current and projected local supplier capability and capacity. This has enabled PROMINP to understand where Brazilian suppliers (i) are already capable; (ii) where they could be capable if supported by international contractors and manufacturers through alliances; and (iii) where there is no current competitive local capability, and thus a need to attract direct foreign investment.

This analysis has fed through into the contracting strategies of Petrobras. For category (ii) above, these strategies intended to incentivise foreign contractors to partner with Brazilian firms to strengthen local capacity: for example, in marine vessel fabrication, cranes and valve manufacture and engineering services. For category (iii), the strategies intended to encourage international firms to establish subsidiaries in Brazil, e.g. to manufacture centrifugal compressors, diesel engines and instrumentation equipment.

Further, for category (iii) the contracting strategies provide incentives to foreign contractors by bundling together work packages and using repeatable designs: for example, in the construction of floating production, storage and offloading (FPSO) vessels and manufacture of certain materials and equipment. It is anticipated that such strategies will increase the returns and reduce the commercial risks for foreign contractors and manufacturers willing to invest in Brazil.

a   PROMINP: O&G Brazilian Industry Mobilisation Programme, London, 15 September 2009; www.ukenergyexcellence.com/marketing-your-business/tools/link_past-events/2009/brasil-energy1-html, accessed 13 June 2011.

# Procurement-driven solutions

Assuming that 'place'—interpreted as the level of local content or a focus on local supplier development—is a material consideration in a client's overall approach to procurement, then what are the possible strategies? Core are: (i) the way in which contracts are packaged; (ii) the extent of client control over the supply chain; and (iii) the choice of compensation arrangement.

## Packaging of contracts

Whether a client elects to procure goods and services as a series of small contracts, or to package work together into higher-value, more encompassing contracts, will impact on the amount of local content or supplier development that can be achieved. The strategic choice is essentially between contract **bundling** and **unbundling**.

**Unbundling** of expenditure into smaller work packages may be preferable for expenditure categories where market surveys or testing has indicated that domestic suppliers can satisfy client demand at the right price, schedule, quality and quantity (i.e. the 'Routine' quadrant of the adapted Kraljic matrix).

Beyond increasing the proportion of local content, there are other reasons why a client might unbundle contracts, and thus strengthen the case for such a procurement strategy. Most obvious is where the client wishes to have clear visibility of potential interface risks and bottlenecks in its supply chain, and thus have direct control over the delivery and quality performance of these suppliers. Since such risks may arise from pressure to use domestic suppliers, unbundling can also be viewed as a strategy to manage expenditure that falls within the 'Appetite' quadrant of the adapted Kraljic matrix.

If the client is heavily dependent on lead contractors to undertake procurement on its behalf, then (if within the bounds of applicable competition rules)[3] the procurement strategy for these catego-

---

3  In some countries competition rules would preclude such a flow-down clause, since the client may be prohibited from directing subcontracting terms to its lead contractors.

ries may include a commitment to include flow-down provision on unbundling within the contract terms for the lead contractors.

Although unbundling as a procurement strategy is likely to increase the proportion of total expenditure awarded to domestic suppliers, it is not always effective in developing labour skills, building supplier capability and long-term competitiveness or managing the commercial risks posed by inexperienced local suppliers. This may be better served by bundling. **Bundling** of contracts takes two main forms:

- **Vertical bundling**. The same contractor is selected to implement a common activity (be that engineering design *or* construction *or* commissioning) across multiple components of a project or operation (production unit, utilities infrastructure, civil works, pipelines, etc.)

- **Horizontal bundling**. The same contractor takes a single component of the project or operations and implements some or all of the relevant activities: design, procurement, construction, commissioning. EPC and EPIC contractors fall into this category

Figure 3.5 shows a hypothetical procurement strategy for an FPSO (floating production, storage and offloading) vessel and associated SURF infrastructure (subsea umbilicals risers and flowlines).

In this scenario the FPSO is destined for an offshore field in an emerging economy. The country is not yet a member of the World Trade Organisation and is thus able to place contractual requirements on the client company to meet local content targets. The country has some existing capability in shipbuilding (relevant skills and shipyards), and its government has ambitious plans to leverage the energy exploration and development sector to develop the local shipbuilding industry so that it can eventually compete in regional markets.

Figure 3.5 **Hypothetical procurement strategy illustrating bundling and unbundling of work packages: FPSO construction in an emerging economy**

Source: Adapted from: G. Stewart, 'The Great Plutonio FPSO: Mixed Contracting Strategies to Optimise Delivery', paper presented at OTC, Houston, TX, May 2008.

| Procurement strategy | FPSO | | SURF |
| --- | --- | --- | --- |
| | Hull | Topsides | |
| Project management | Client | | |
| Detailed engineering | Domestic EPC with international consulting engineer | International EPCm | International EPIC Tendering and compensation incentives for inward investment |
| Procurement | | | |
| Fabrication | | | |
| Transportation of hull | Domestic subcontractor | | |
| Integration | | | |
| Installation | | | |
| Commissioning | | | |
| Start-up | Client | | |

The resulting procurement strategy is formulated to raise the volume of local content in the project (proportion of spend with domestic suppliers), while concurrently managing the cost, schedule and quality risks of so doing, *and* aligning with government ambitions for developing a competitive shipbuilding industry.

The product is a 'mixed' procurement strategy, combining elements of both vertical and horizontal contract bundling as well as unbundling. The engineering design, procurement, fabrication, integration, installation and commissioning of SURF infrastructure is under a single EPIC contract, tendered to experienced international contractors. Bundling the work in this way incentivises the winning contractor to use its influence over its suppliers of SURF equipment to encourage them to set up product finishing, maintenance and repair facilities in the host country (a strategy that fits the 'Critical' quadrant of the adapted Kraljic matrix).

To achieve this outcome, the procurement strategy establishes the principle of giving additional weight in the EPIC tender evaluation to bidders able to leverage this type of investment. Highest weighting is given to inward investment in those categories of equipment manufacture and repair services most closely aligned with the host government's ambitions for technology transfer and industrial development.

In contrast, the proposed procurement strategy for FPSO construction is to partially unbundle. The FPSO topsides engineering, procurement and construction management services are separated from the subcontracted fabrication work under an EPCm (engineering, procurement, construction-management) lump-sum contract. The total work package is tendered to experienced international contractors, but with the pricing of the subcontract for fabrication, integration and commissioning work negotiated with the preferred bidder as an open-book build-up to lump sum.

This approach provides the client with evidence that the necessary level of risk mitigation is priced in (either directly within the lump sum or as an option or contingency), such as additional in-the-yard management supervision and quality control. The procurement strategy further requires that tendering for the EPCm contract should stipulate that the tenderer must choose between a limited number of pre-market-tested, nominated, local fabrication subcontractors. In addition, overall project management for the fabrication and integration work is retained by the client to further manage the schedule and quality risks involved in using less experienced local fabricators.

With regard to the FPSO hull, design, procurement and fabrication is isolated from the topsides work, enabling experienced shipbuilders in the country to bid directly for the work. To manage the inherent risks the procurement strategy requires that an experienced engineering consultant firm be part of the bidding consortium. This firm will contribute the design drawings and provide contract performance oversight. As with the EPCm contract, the client also retains an overarching project management role.

A survey of the local fabrication and shipbuilding yards suggested the need for prior capital investment in earth works, heavy equipment and experienced project managers. To incentivise these investments, the procurement strategy includes a stated presumption to place additional orders for FPSO construction in the same local yards, if contract performance targets on the first FPSO are met. This presumption is to be communicated to the tenderers along with

Box 3.2 **Procurement strategy to manage supplier risks and build competitiveness**

**An illustration from Trinidad**

From 2003, BG Trinidad and Tobago executed a contracting strategy formulated in part to ensure that fabrication of its offshore platforms (deck and jacket) could be performed by a Trinidadian fabricator. Key elements of the strategy were:

- A replicable, *cookie-cutter*, design for the platform jacket and deck, such that the local fabricator could move up the learning curve on progressive platforms
- A price premium, paid in part to cover the additional shipping costs of importing construction materials to enable fabrication in Trinidad, additional insurance costs and competence development of the fabricator's employees
- A decision-gate within the series of platform constructions to ensure adequate performance by the fabricator before award of subsequent platforms

The local fabricator, TOFCO Ltd, successfully completed the Cannonball platform in 2005 and was subsequently awarded contracts to construct a sequence of additional platforms on a rolling basis.

In 2006, the operations of BG Group in Trinidad formulated its contracting strategy to construct and install a new platform on the Poinsettia offshore field. To align with the industrial policy objectives of the government and to protect commercial interests, a core objective of the contracting strategy was to maximise local content through alliances between the winning international EPCm contractor and a Trinidadian deck fabricator. The strategy led to:

- Local content being an important and communicated evaluation criterion
- The letter of award to the EPCm contractor specifically nominating TOFCO as the fabricator of the platform deck
- An **open-book** approach to agree a lump-sum contract with the EPC contractor, needed to provide comfort that the risks posed by TOFCO were fully mitigated and priced in
- Prior to contract execution, capital investment by TOFCO in site development, equipment and marine vessel capability

BG was thus able to procure the topsides of the Poinsettia platform from TOFCO. At 4,200 tonnes, this deck was three times the weight of the previous BP decks. The subcontract achieved 91% local content (measured as economic value added to the Trinidadian economy) and significantly developed the capability and competitiveness of the fabricator, especially in HSSE performance and project controls (details of this illustration are given in Chapter 4).

the key performance indicators that will trigger the follow-on work: schedule delivery, labour productivity rates, quality of project management, HSSE (health, safety, security, environment) performance and welding defects performance.

In summary then, with reference to Figure 3.5, unbundling seems likely to work best where there is existing domestic supplier capability, and/or measures can readily be put in place to overcome gaps such that the procuring entity has the appetite to take on the risks involved (the 'Routine' and 'Appetite' quadrants of Figure 3.4). Bundling is likely to be preferable in cases where more substantive building of the capability of domestic suppliers is needed, either because of concern over serious risks to schedule or quality (the 'Critical' quadrant), or where the risks are low but there is some reputational or long-term cost advantage to strengthening the competitiveness of local suppliers (the 'Leverage' quadrant).

Box 3.2 illustrates this type of leveraged procurement strategy in the context of oil field platform fabrication in Trinidad and Tobago. Chapter 4 is dedicated to an analysis of this case study.

## Control over the supply chain

The level of commercial risk consequent of sourcing from domestic suppliers in different expenditure categories will inform the extent to which the client wishes to stay in management control of its local procurement. For example, with reference to the further adapted Kraljic matrix in Figure 3.6, for local suppliers proven by market testing to be capable and competitive on the other four 'rights', the client may elect to use a procurement strategy that procures from these local suppliers using standardised contract terms and which states the scope of work or goods for purchase as standardised performance requirements. In such cases no additional client supervision is needed, nor the introduction of some higher-tier contractor or consulting engineer to provide additional supervision. Procurement strategies need to be well informed of exactly where within the expenditure plans such opportunities arise, since procuring from these suppliers will likely constitute a high proportion of the total contributions to local content.

Figure 3.6 **Procurement strategy choices for packaging of works, client control and compensation arrangements**

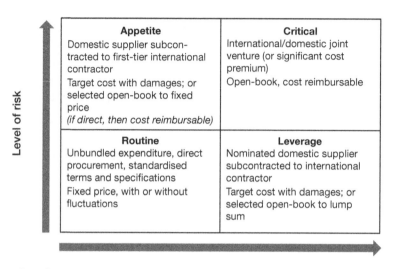

| | **Appetite** | **Critical** |
|---|---|---|
| **Level of risk** ↑ | Domestic supplier subcontracted to first-tier international contractor<br><br>Target cost with damages; or selected open-book to fixed price<br>*(if direct, then cost reimbursable)* | International/domestic joint venture (or significant cost premium)<br><br>Open-book, cost reimbursable |
| | **Routine** | **Leverage** |
| | Unbundled expenditure, direct procurement, standardised terms and specifications<br><br>Fixed price, with or without fluctuations | Nominated domestic supplier subcontracted to international contractor<br><br>Target cost with damages; or selected open-book to lump sum |

Local content      →      **Supplier development**

The case is different for goods and services for which local suppliers either present a significant but manageable risk (the Appetite quadrant), or offer opportunity to develop local supplier capability (the Leverage quadrant). It is rational for clients who are compelled to procure from inefficient or inexperienced state-owned or local private suppliers to insert between themselves and the domestic supplier a lead contractor or consultant engineer. Procurement strategies need to identify which spend categories might be relevant to this approach, what the level of risk or opportunity is, and describe the core principles for contract award to manage the risks or realise the opportunities, whether contested tender, negotiated contract or single sourced. Crucially, the strategy needs to articulate what the purpose of the higher-tier contractor is with respect to supporting local suppliers, whether that is to:

- **Safeguard contract performance** (e.g. through additional quality controls, management supervision, third party inspections)

- **Develop supplier potential** (e.g. enabling suppliers to achieve international quality standards, investing in joint ventures, facilitating long-term technology transfer or providing access to regional or global markets)

- Or **some combination**, as with long-term or repeat contracts that facilitate a learning curve relevant to both immediate contract performance and future marketability

With specific regard to the level of client control over expenditure in the Critical quadrant, here the commercial risks are likely to be so great that the procurement strategy needs to establish the general principles of contract award, be that to:

- Accept a **cost premium** to mitigate the additional risks or provide insurance (e.g. a backup contract with an alternative supplier, or financial insurance)

- Require specified **liquidated damages** as a condition of contract

- Accept a **delay to supply** delivery or project schedule to enable the capability of domestic suppliers to be enhanced to more competitive acceptable levels of performance

- Limit tender lists only to where an internationally experienced contractor enters into a **joint venture** with a relevant domestic supplier (and in such a way that the international contractor carries the main contractual risks and liabilities)

## Compensation arrangements

The procurement strategy will also need to consider how best to use compensation payments to limit the risks of local sourcing, and/or how to incentivise contractors to meet local content targets or achieve successful supplier development.

In reference to Figure 3.6, direct expenditure with a domestic supplier in the moderately risky Appetite quadrant is more likely to benefit from a cost reimbursable compensation structure, payable against a schedule of rates or more detailed bill of quantities.

Where an experienced international contractor is providing higher-tier management of domestic suppliers, then for expenditure falling within either the Appetite or Leverage quadrants, there are likely two main compensation options applicable to the lead contractor:

- For less risky local suppliers, **target cost** (e.g. 50/50 pain gain), with **liquidated damages** against schedule slippage

- For more risky local suppliers, selective **open-book** build-up of cost, allowing scrutiny over the riskiest supplier and subcontractor contracts

The assumptions in both cases are that the international contractor will wish to retain some element of cost control and 'upside' over the type and quality of support it gives to domestic suppliers, and that the client has sufficient confidence to allow the contractor to take on such risks.

For expenditure in the Critical quadrant, the procurement strategy is likely to favour an **open-book, cost-reimbursable** mechanism, to minimise the risks involved.

## Conclusions

Purchasing goods and services from the right 'place' is becoming an increasingly important consideration in the formulation of procurement strategies. Give insufficient weight to regulatory and political expectations for the local sourcing of goods and services and supplier development and compliance targets may be missed, eligibility to recover expenditure costs forgone, and opportunities for enhanced reputation lost. Give too much, and serious commercial value can be eroded because of the higher costs of goods and services, longer delivery times and inferior quality.

Knowing what should constitute an effective procurement strategy to meet expectations around local content requires some key considerations:

- An understanding of the **level of risk** posed by local suppliers in different expenditure categories

- The right choices on packaging expenditure through contract **bundling and unbundling**

- Placing experienced contractors between the client and riskier local suppliers

- Establishing principles of **contractor selection** and using the leverage afforded by **scale** and repeat work to incentivise lead contractors to play a pivotal role in local supply chain oversight and supplier development

- Adopting a **compensation** structure suited to the level of risk of local suppliers and the client's objectives for local sourcing and supplier development

# 4

# Case study

## Procurement as a driver of national competitiveness in the Poinsettia project, BG Group, Trinidad and Tobago

This chapter is published with the kind permission of BG Group. The chapter was originally prepared under commission by the author, as part of BG Group's contribution to the National Market Participation Initiative of the World Business Council for Sustainable Development. In preparing this text the author interviewed the main stakeholders in the Poinsettia project, both the relevant project and procurement managers within BG Group and managers and workers at the TOFCO fabrication yard. The text also draws on experiences of the author before joining BG Group as a consultant to BP Trinidad and Tobago.

# Context

## BG Group operations in Trinidad and Tobago

BG Group has been operating in Trinidad and Tobago since 1989, and is a key gas producer in the country. BG Group currently supplies gas to the domestic market and to Atlantic LNG. In 2008, approximately two-thirds of production was exported as LNG with the remainder going to the domestic market.

BG Group is the operator of two offshore blocks in Trinidad and Tobago: the East Coast Marine Area, where it manages production from the Dolphin gas field, and the North Coast Marine Area (NCMA), which includes six gas fields, including the Poinsettia field.

In December 2000, the Government of Trinidad and Tobago approved the development of the first three fields in the NCMA. These fields are being developed in four phases to supply gas to Atlantic LNG Trains 2, 3 and 4. Phase 3c in the development of the NCMA included a new drilling and production platform on the Poinsettia field, tied back to a pre-drilled well, and connected by a 20 inch pipe to the existing BG Hibiscus platform. This phase is now complete and in production.

## The Poinsettia platform

The Poinsettia platform increased processing capability by BG Group in Trinidad and Tobago by 350 million scfd (standard cubic feet/day) of natural gas, a rise of a third from its then current capacity of 1 billion scfd. In January 2009 the first gas flowed through the new platform on time and on budget. This was despite the most inflationary and competitive exploration and production supplier market for more than a generation, as well as 69 days lost on the project's critical path time due to strikes, weather standby and *force majeure*.

The Poinsettia platform consisted of a 168-metre-high, 10,000 tonne jacket fabricated on the Gulf Coast of the USA, and a 4,200 tonne deck (topsides) constructed in Trinidad. Plate 4.1 shows the moment when the jacket was positioned in place.

Plate 4.1 **Positioning of the Poinsettia platform jacket**

The topsides for the platform were designed to accommodate a 6,000 tonne drilling rig. This rig was transferred to Poinsettia from BG Group's Dolphin field off Trinidad's east coast for a two-year drilling programme commencing in mid-2009.

The Poinsettia topsides were constructed almost entirely at the fabrication facility of a Trinidadian-registered company, TOFCO Ltd, located on the LABIDCO industrial estate at La Brea, on the west coast of Trinidad.

## TOFCO: local fabricator

TOFCO is a 50/50 joint venture between Contractors (CMC) of Louisiana, USA, with construction facilities in Harvey and Houma, and Welfab Limited, a Trinidadian services company. Welfab Ltd has been in operation since 1979 from its Claxton Bay base.

It is important to note that the Poinsettia topsides are by no means the first large fabrication contract to be won by TOFCO and constructed at its facility. TOFCO itself owes its origins in part to a decision by BP in Trinidad (BPTT) to place orders for a series of jackets and decks in Trinidad, starting in 2006 with the 'Cannonball' project. BPTT were commended by the government at the time for this decision.

The BP platforms are a series of moderate-sized, 'cookie-cutter', decks and jackets, weighing around 850 tonnes and 950 tonnes, respectively (the Poinsettia topsides are four times this weight). In addition to a number of smaller fabrication works, TOFCO also won work from EOG to construct the Oil Bird platform (a 1,000 tonne deck and 1,300 tonne jacket) and the deck for its Toucan platform. At one point in 2007 four jobs were running simultaneously at the fabrication yard: the BP Savonette deck and jacket, BG Group's Poinsettia topsides and EOG's Toucan deck. Plate 4.2 shows construction of the Poinsettia topsides taking place at the TOFCO fabrication facility concurrently with the deck and jacket for the BP Savonette platform.

Plate 4.2 **Concurrent construction of the BG Group Poinsettia topsides with BP deck and jacket**

In constructing the Poinsettia topsides, TOFCO took responsibilities both on- and offshore, as follows:

- **Onshore**. Structural fabrication; construction; installation of gas and diesel generators, installation of electrical equipment, instrumentation, 20 km of cable and 5 km piping; painting; non-destructive testing; pre-commissioning, load out and seafastening

- **Offshore**. Sixty-two workers from TOFCO housed for two months in temporary accommodation on the Poinsettia platform to execute the final hook-up and commissioning phases

# Government local content policy

In 2006/7, when feasibility studies on Phase 3c of the NCMA began, the stated policy of the Government of the Republic of Trinidad and Tobago on local content was to 'strongly encourage but not mandate'. An influential policy document, the *Local Content and Local Participation Policy and Framework*,[1] was published in 2006, and the Permanent Local Content Committee (PLCC) established by the Energy Ministry to oversee policy delivery. This policy sets a clear imperative for operators to maximise local content and build the capabilities of domestic suppliers. The policy document makes the case as follows:

> In seeking to achieve developed nation status, Trinidad and Tobago has to move to a position of increased GNP vs. GDP and of producing higher value-added goods and services for export. The energy sector provides excellent opportunities, so to do, but these are only achieved through increased local participation in the value chain. Current levels of local value capture are in the 10% range and increasing this will have a significant impact on the national economy.

Specifically the policy called on operators to support three types of measure:

- **Local participation**. Maximise the depth and breadth of local ownership, control and financing, in order to increase

---

1 Government of Trinidad and Tobago, 'Local Content and Local Participation Policy and Framework', 2004, Ministry of Energy and Energy Industries, Permanent Local Content Committee; www.energy.gov.tt/content/72.pdf, accessed 23 June 2011.

local value-capture from all parts of the value chain created from the resource, including those activities in which T&T people, businesses and capital are not currently engaged, both within and outside of T&T

- **Local content**. Maximise the level of usage of local goods and services, people, businesses and financing

- **Local capability development**. Maximise the impact of the ongoing sector activities, through the transfer of technology and know-how to:
    - Enhance, deepen and broaden the capability and international competitiveness of T&T's people and businesses within the sector
    - Create and enhance capabilities that are transferable to other sectors within T&T
    - Create and support cluster developments with other industries that have a natural synergy with the energy sector and which may have the capacity to diversify and/ or sustain the economy after the resource is depleted

Fabrication of the Poinsettia platform topsides at TOFCO had a positive impact on all three of these policy areas.

Critically, operators were required to report on the levels of local content they achieved, although no minimum targets were set. The key metric for this reporting was 'the value of supply chain expenditure with suppliers registered in Trinidad and Tobago'. This metric provided an incentive for international contractors to invest in the country and establish subsidiaries. The permitting regime at the time further encouraged these subsidiaries to employ Trinidadian workers, based on a presumption in favour of nationals over non-nationals unless a particular skill or managerial shortfall could be proven.

# Risks of local fabrication

Seeking to maximise local content in a country with limited capabilities in oil field development services is not without risk. For the Poinsettia project, the primary risks were to schedule, cost and worker safety.

## Schedule risks

A key question facing BG Group in the inception stage of Phase 3c was as follows: 'if effort is made to utilise locally owned companies, increase local content and build local supplier capability and competitiveness, will this delay the target date for gas production?' The highly competitive market for gas field services at the time offered BG Group and its partners only a narrow window of opportunity to exercise an option on a heavy-lift vessel owned by J Ray McDermott, an international maritime construction company. The vessel was needed to install the platform. A failure by TOFCO to complete the topsides on time would therefore have affected BG Group and its partners in Trinidad by raising costs and would delay the flow of revenues from production.

Risks to the project schedule from electing to nominate TOFCO as the platform subcontractor were assessed by BG Group. These included:

- **Welding performance**. Though the quality of welding by workers at TOFCO was credible (as proven on a series of platform for BP), productivity was potentially lower than that achieved on the Gulf Coast of the USA

- **Industrial disputes**. The risk of industrial disputes that could delay the project and/or add to its cost (TOFCO had experienced just such disputes in the recent past with workers from the nearby La Brea community, and indeed the contract was affected by a short strike by TOFCO workers)

- **Weather**. Without covered sheds sufficient to protect construction work from the elements, there was a risk that 'extraordinary' weather (i.e. very heavy rainfall) might delay work

The EPIC (engineering, procurement, installation and commissioning) contract contained incentives for the mechanical completion of the platform (deck and jacket) in its offshore location. This included performance incentives for early completion and capped liquidated damages for late completion. The contract allowed for a window of 60 days between the end of positive incentives and the start of liquidated damages. This provided flexibility to accommodate delays that might arise owing to the types of risk identified above. In the event, it seems that a proportion of this period of flexibility was indeed consumed by adverse weather and strike action at the TOFCO facility. The precise details are unclear but, despite these delays, overall mechanical completion was achieved against the project schedule.

## Cost risks

In general, although elevating local content in procurement expenditure is an opportunity for long-term reductions in operational (and potentially project) costs, in the short term such initiatives can be more expensive. For example, it is understood that BP supported a premium for its initial platforms to be fabricated in Trinidad,[2] but that, by using a repeatable design, compensation incentives and close management support, premiums for subsequent platforms were able to fall over time.

The key test for BG Group was whether the topsides for the Poinsettia platform could be built at a comparable cost to that which could be achieved internationally. To investigate this question, BG Group conducted a study of the relative costs and benefits of constructing the Poinsettia topsides in Trinidad, compared with the US Gulf Coast (the most likely alternative). The study concluded no material difference in total cost. It showed that the costs that would incur to BG Group and its partners from additional management support and lower productivity (e.g. welding rates) consequent of subcontracting to TOFCO, would be offset by the benefits of lower

2 University of the West Indies, 'BP Trinidad and Tobago Limited', 2005, Arthur Lok Jack Graduate School of Business, University of the West Indies, Trinidad, MCS-CSR-05-05; https://www.menas.co.uk/App_Data/elib/bptt.pdf, accessed 23 June 2011.

transportation costs (freight and insurance costs of moving the top-sides across the hurricane-prone Gulf of Mexico) and a lower average cost of labour.

## Safety risks

There were also risks identified around worker health and safety. In particular, with TOFCO anticipated to take on 400 additional workers to cope with the combined BG Group and BP workload during the period 2007 and 2008, there would be an increased risk of incidences of injuries.

# Role of procurement to manage risks and build competitiveness

Key to the decision to construct the Poinsettia topsides in Trinidad has been the way in which the different stages in contracting the NCMA Phase 3c project have been conducted. The NCMA Phase 3c project was executed through a single major EPIC contract, placed with a consortium comprising Fluor Enterprises and J Ray McDermott. The EPIC contract involved: engineering, procurement, construction, load out and seafasten, transport and installation, hook-up and commissioning support. Specific criteria and provisions were introduced into the project contracting strategy, tender documents and contracts, designed to maximise local content, build supplier competitiveness and manage the associated risks and costs.

Government local content policy was factored into the procurement process from the start. One of the key drivers in the contracting strategy for Phase 3c was the 'maximisation of local Trinidad content . . . this being achieved by . . . having international companies aligning local capabilities . . . providing [that] the project requirements are met and the budget and schedule are assured'. The principle was thus established that there would be no cost premium for work on the project carried out in Trinidad. This is an important consideration, since it meant that any participating Trinidadian-owned company would, on completion of its work, be able to market itself in the future as having had experience on a major project on an 'internationally competitive' basis.

Following a pre-qualification process with a number of consortia, in which local content was a key evaluative criterion, it was decided to single-source the main EPIC contract. The inflationary and highly competitive supplier market at the time meant that a full competitive tender ran the risk of both pricing in cost escalations and delaying the project. To manage the risks posed by single sourcing, the post award negotiations took place as a fully transparent 'open-book' audit of the contract price and rates for variations. This was advantageous to the consideration of local content. An open-book approach ensured transparency over both the total value of work the contractor intended to conduct in Trinidad and the adequacy of measures taken to manage the associated risks.

In the Letter of Award to Fluor Enterprises and JRM, TOFCO was nominated as the subcontractor for construction of the Poinsettia topsides. Back at pre-qualification stage, it had been thought that TOFCO might form part of the lead contractor consortium with Fluor and JRM. Given the high value of the EPIC contract, and the need for the lead contractors to be 'jointly and severally liable', it was necessary to forgo this proposal. Other types of contract formulation were also considered, including managing the contract as an EPCm (engineering, procurement and construction-management) arrangement, with TOFCO contracted directly by BG Trinidad and Tobago. However, better mitigation of construction risk was felt to lie with the closer management and oversight that would come if the consortium of Fluor Enterprises and JRM were held contractually liable for construction as well as engineering and procurement.

Table 4.1 identifies the main criteria and provisions introduced into the procurement process for the NCMA Phase 3c project, intended to facilitate local fabrication of the Poinsettia platform topsides while managing the risks.

Table 4.1  **Role of NCMA Phase 3c procurement process in facilitating local content**

| Stage in process | Key criteria and provisions |
| --- | --- |
| Feasibility study | BG Group provides sufficient information to TOFCO to enable it to demonstrate capability to construct Poinsettia topsides |
| Contracting strategy | 'Maximisation of local Trinidad content . . .' one of three key drivers in contracting strategy. '. . . this being achieved by . . . having international companies aligning local capabilities . . . providing the project requirements are met and the budget and schedule are assured' |
| Pre-qualification | Letter of invitation to pre-tender contractors/ consortia indicates that local content is a key evaluative criterion |
| Market survey | Encouraged international/local teaming arrangements whereby a single consortium would cover all aspects of project delivery |
| Cost–benefit study | Study demonstrated no material difference in overall cost/benefit between Trinidad and Gulf Coast |
| Investment committee | Given distorted market conditions, single sourcing decision taken. Subsequent 'open-book' build up of lump sum facilitated more effective inclusion of local content considerations |
| Letter of award | Letter of award nominates TOFCO as subcontractor |
| EPIC contract provisions | Under EPIC contract, liabilities for TOFCO completing the topsides laid with the Fluor/RJD consortium |
| | *Force majeure* unusually included local or national strikes and industrial disputes, in part to acknowledge TOFCO's concern that such disputes could be politically motivated and thus outside its control |

# Local content outcomes

## Local content across the project

Analysis by BG Group of the impact of expenditure on the NCMA Phase 3c shows that approximately 21% of total spend went in either wages to Trinidadian nationals or contracts to companies registered in Trinidad and Tobago. Highlights are given in Figure 4.1 with details in Table 4.2. In summary:

- 58% of **pre-sanction** costs went to Trinidadian-registered contractors, including 100% of FEED to Fluor Daniel SA Ltd, Port of Spain, and 100% of geotechnical and geophysical costs

- 51% of **owner management** costs, including 32% of project management team costs and 100% of general and administrative costs

- 40% of total costs for engineering, procurement, construction, installation and commissioning of the **Poinsettia topsides**, with 100% of construction, installation, hook-up and commissioning to TOFCO Ltd

- 18% of costs on **pipelines and subsea** works, including 65% of diving services to Caldive/Helix

## Local content in topsides construction

In accordance with the reporting requirements at the time, local content was calculated as the proportion of expenditure contracted to Trinidadian-registered firms. Since TOFCO is registered in Trinidad, and construction of the topsides was a single subcontract, so local content for the topsides was 100%.

A more accurate measure of local content, and one used by BG Group, is the actual value contributed (AVC) to the domestic economy arising from procurement. In the NCMA Phase 3c project, the largest single subcontract to a nationally registered supplier was to TOFCO Ltd for the construction and installation of the Poinsettia topsides. The subcontract included both services and procurement

page 96 ➔

Figure 4.1 **Local content highlights in Phase 3c, Poinsettia project, Trinidad and Tobago**

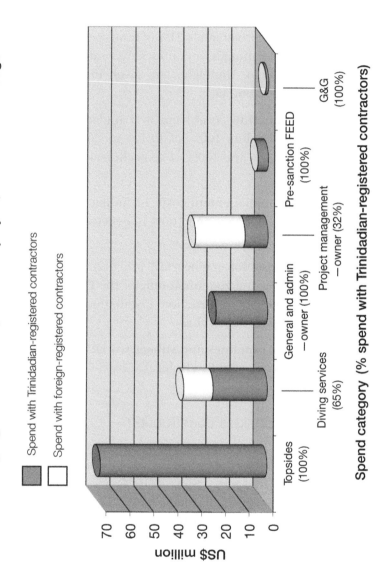

G&G, geosciences and geophysics

Table 4.2 **Local content as % of expenditure with contractors registered in Trinidad and Tobago**

| NCMA Phase 3c | Spend categories | **Local content (%)** As value of contracts placed with contractors registered in Trinidad | **Cost weighted** |
|---|---|---|---|
| **Pre-sanction costs** | | **58.0%** | **1.4%** |
| | 2005 PM | 36.8% | 0.3% |
| | Geotechnical and geophysical | 100.0% | 0.1% |
| | FEED | 100.0% | 0.5% |
| | 2006 PM | 48.9% | 0.3% |
| **Owner costs: management costs** | | **51.2%** | **4.1%** |
| | PMT costs | 32.1% | 1.2% |
| | Port of Spain support: including general and admin | 100.0% | 2.6% |
| | Consultancy and rental (Wood Group) | 90.5% | 0.2% |
| Owner costs: logistics | | **100.0%** | **0.8%** |
| **Owner costs: third-party contracts** | | **21.0%** | **0.3%** |
| | Helicopters | 100.0% | 0.3% |
| | Supply boats | 100.0% | 0.1% |
| Owner costs: car insurance | | **6.0%** | **0.1%** |
| **Poinsettia topsides** | | **40.0%** | **8.3%** |
| | Lump sum | 43.3% | 8.3% |
| | Provisional sum | | |
| | Identified growth | | |
| | Approved variations | | |
| | Pending variations (including PS adj) | | |
| Poinsettia jacket | | **0.0%** | **0.0%** |
| Poinsettia installation | Transport and installation | **1.2%** | **0.1%** |

| NCMA Phase 3c | Spend categories | Local content (%) As value of contracts placed with contractors registered in Trinidad | Cost weighted |
|---|---|---|---|
| Hibiscus modifications | | **34.8%** | **1.0%** |
| | Construction management and field management | 25.4% | 0.3% |
| | Equipment and bulk | 13.1% | 0.1% |
| | Installation: work performed locally | 100.0% | 0.6% |
| Pipelines and subsea | | **18.3%** | **3.5%** |
| | Caldive/Helix – JV – registered for VAT | **64.5%** | **2.7%** |
| Subsea trees and control | | **0.0%** | **0.0%** |
| Drilling | | 7.0% | 1.4% |
| Total base cost | | | **21.1%** |

of equipment and materials. Measured by AVC, the highest proportion of local content within the subcontract was for fabrication and structural work (100% AVC, representing 54% of total contract value). Across the subcontract, BG Trinidad and Tobago estimate that 91.3% of the total value of the TOFCO subcontract stayed in the Trinidadian economy. This includes:

- Fabrication and structural work (100% AVC, 54% of contract value)

- Construction management support (55% AVC, 3% of contract value)

- Marine vessels (100% AVC, 5% of contract value)

- Electrical and instrumentation costs (59% AVC, 7% of contract value)

- Load out and seafasten costs (100% AVC, 3% of contract value)

In addition, it is estimated that 99% of the 1.1 million hours worked on the Poinsettia topsides were undertaken by Trinidadian nationals.

Of these, 27% of the labour came from the nearby La Brea community and approximately 50% from within five miles.

## Improvements in local industrial capability and competitiveness

Bidding for and winning the Poinsettia topsides subcontract was material to TOFCO taking decisions to make new capital investments in its fabrication facilities and improve its internal HSSE and project control processes.

### New capital investment and improved processes

As already noted, construction work on the 4,200 tonne Poinsettia topsides coincided with two other substantial contracts for TOFCO: the 850 tonne BP Savonette platform and 900 tonne jacket, and EOG's Toucan topsides at 1,580 tonnes. The expectation of an increased volume of work in a concentrated time period promoted new capital investment by TOFCO. This included the purchase of new cranes, forklift trucks, compressors, lighting towers and welding machines. To hold the weight of the Poinsettia platform, investments were made to reinforce the soil under the construction zone with concrete piles.

Also significant has been investment by TOFCO in the refurbishment of a supply boat and standby vessel, and the operation of these from the La Brea site (and from EOG's supply base at Chag) to service the installation, hook-up and commissioning of the Poinsettia topsides. This was the first time that attempts had been made to develop a permanent marine vessel support base in Trinidad. The investment represented a step forward for the government in achieving its ambition for Trinidad to develop an indigenous fleet of vessels to support its offshore fields.

### Worker safety reporting

Obligations in the subcontract with the Fluor/JRM consortium included requirements on TOFCO to improve its performance and reporting on worker safety. Around 400 new workers arrived on the TOFCO site during the construction period. With this arrival came an increased risk of injuries. To manage the risk, BG Group and Fluor provided HSE (health, safety and environment) management support to TOFCO and additional HSE training to strengthen its reporting regime. In the 12 months prior to sail-away of the topsides in November 2008, TOFCO's reported data was able to show:

- Zero lost-time injuries (lost-time injury frequency, LTIF, see Fig. 4.2) reported for the period of Poinsettia construction

- A rolling average total recordable incident frequency (TRIF) per million hours to November 2008 of 0.97; the BG Group target for 2008 was 1.35 (refer to Fig. 4.2)

- A rolling average of 80 first aid cases (FAC) per million hours to November 2008 (a slightly larger fabrication yard in the Middle East achieved a rate of 85 in the same period. For construction of the Poinsettia jacket at the J Ray McDermott's construction yard in Morgan City on the Gulf Coast the rate was 50). The rise in first aid cases can clearly be linked to a management directive for workers to report minor cases (refer to Fig. 4.3)

Figure 4.2 **Trend in safety performance at TOFCO over contract period: LTIF and TRIF**

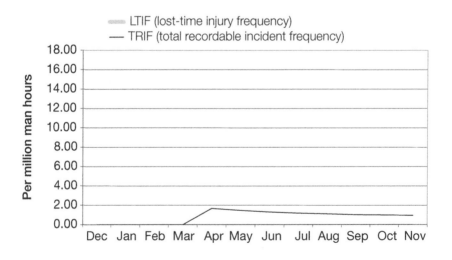

Figure 4.3 **Trend in safety performance at TOFCO over contract period: rolling first aid case rate, 2008**

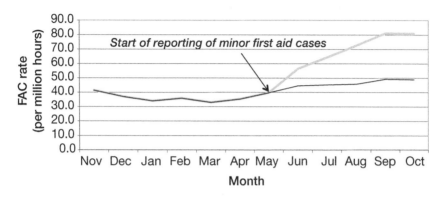

Following installation of the platform, 62 workers from TOFCO spent over a month offshore undertaking hook-up and commissioning work. This is complex and dangerous labour and few of the TOFCO workers had experienced such a working environment before. It is testament to the skill of these men, to the HSSE management by TOFCO, and to the management support provided by BG T&T and Fluor that this offshore work experienced zero lost-time injuries and only one first aid injury.

For such a young company, TOFCO's offshore and onshore safety record on the Poinsettia topsides contract, and its own improvements in safety reporting, will be key factors in its ability to compete in international tenders in the years ahead. This record on safety is also central to TOFCO's reputation within Trinidad and Tobago itself. As Suresh Gangabissoon, General Manager at TOFCO, points out, 'if we fail to deliver on safety, the whole island will know about it'.

The complexity of the scope of work for the Poinsettia topsides, combined with the work on two other jobs taking place at the same time, led TOFCO to invest in new project management competences and tools, including Prima Vera software. But as Suresh Gangabissoon points out, 'it's not all about software, it's also the management skills needed to map out the required competencies with the men on the ground and then plan resourcing accordingly'.

# Prospects for future marketing

The test for success of local content development initiatives is not simply the proportion of supply chain expenditure spent with locally registered contractors, or even the proportion of spend staying within the domestic economy. What is equally important to local industrial development, if not more so, is whether in the process of executing a contract the local supplier develops capabilities and capacity to be more competitive in the future.

Taken together, the capital investments, improvements in worker safety performance and project management processes, and the track record of meeting a critical schedule deadline on a major international project without subsidies, positions TOFCO favourably against its competition. The company is already marketing itself in Nigeria and Venezuela on the back of the Poinsettia and BP platform work, not only as a competent fabricator, but also as a company that knows what it takes to step up as a local contractor to international standards of performance. 'We will undoubtedly use our new experience in hook-up and commissioning on Poinsettia as a key selling point to market ourselves in the future' (Suresh Gangabissoon, General Manager at TOFCO).

Nearer to home, TOFCO's experience offshore with the hook-up and commissioning of Trinidad's largest platform to date will strengthen the company's bids for similar work in Trinidad as well as remedial work and asset integrity. The latter will be important as the economic challenges facing the oil and gas exploration and development industry are diverting the attention of operators away from new projects and towards 'brownfield work': extending the efficiency and life of their existing assets.

It is not only the new expertise gained by TOFCO on the Poinsettia project that supports the company's future marketing efforts, nor is it the improvements in its capabilities from capital investment and better quality controls; just as important has been the partnering ethos behind the Fluor/JRM/TOFCO arrangement. This arrangement demonstrates that TOFCO can play its part in a type of contracting model that gives operators comfort to subcontract schedule-critical work to a local fabricator. Further, it suggests that TOFCO may be able to take on even more complex scopes of work: for example, constructing topsides that include accommodation units, compression modules and rotating equipment. To this end, BG was clearly satisfied with the overall performance of TOFCO: 'TOFCO have proved themselves . . . never failed to deliver good quality products on time. Now in pole position to win more of this type of work. Would we use them again? Absolutely' (Steve Warner, C&P Manager for NCMA Phase 3c).

'What Poinsettia has done for TOFCO is provide the argument that they *can* do it, that they can step up to more complex and larger scopes of work, and still deliver on time' (Graham Balchin, Project's Director, BG Trinidad and Tobago).

## Conclusions

The objective of this chapter has been to provide an example of how to develop the capacity and competitiveness of a local contractor for the supply of a major component in a development project. The case provides evidence of the following:

- The importance of the **choice of procurement processes** in facilitating local content and the development of supplier capability and competitiveness, while also managing the inherent risks to cost, schedule and quality. In particular:
  - Making local content and supplier development explicit drivers in project **contracting strategies** and **pre-qualification** processes
  - The positive role that can be played by **post-award open-book** negotiations to provide clarity over how contractors and subcontractors will achieve local content and supplier development and manage the associated risks

- The value of conducting prior **assessment of the costs and benefits** of local versus foreign solutions; for example, cost savings on labour and transportation from using local contractors may offset lower productivity and the costs of more intensive construction-management

## Box 4.1 **Lessons on selecting and interpreting local content metrics**

**Certain metrics may not necessarily deliver the perceived levels of local content:**

Contrast the topsides subcontract, which reports 100% local content if crudely measured as a proportion of contract value with a nationally registered company, with 91% if measured as actual value contributed to the domestic economy. Or, more dramatically, the construction and management services component of the same subcontract, which is 100% local content under the crude metric and 55% under the AVC metric.

**Setting high local targets may not result in higher levels of local content:**

In the case of the overall Phase 3c Poinsettia project, even with detailed prior analysis of the capabilities of the domestic supplier market, combined with an intelligent procurement process making it possible to contract a domestic fabricator with no previous experience of this size of topsides, the proportion of the project costs contracted to nationally registered companies was 21%. Would a higher figure have been achieved had the authorities mandated a local content target of, say, 40%? Perhaps the company would have simply accepted the inherent fines, or provided a premium to mitigate the higher risks, or accepted a delay in the schedule to first gas and the subsequent impact of this on commercial returns and government revenues. Or perhaps the company would have found creative ways to meet the target: for example, by requiring foreign companies to establish contract-specific subsidiaries or joint ventures that operated in name only and carried no inward investment or technology transfer.

**Accurate metrics for measuring local content, such as AVC, do not necessarily reflect the level of competitiveness of the national industry:**

It is quite possible, especially if a result of political pressure to preference inexperienced domestic suppliers, that a contract could achieve a very high level of local content but at the same time be overpriced, achieve low levels of labour productivity, be late in delivery of the procured service or goods, injure its workforce and produce work of substandard quality. For local industry to achieve sustainable steps towards international competitiveness, additional metrics are needed which are not usually captured in the standard formulae. As illustrated by the Poinsettia contract, this may include metrics that measure new fixed capital investments arising from contract award and improvements in labour productivity, HSE and quality performance.

- **How partnering arrangements between local subcontractors and international firms** may enable local firms to 'step up' to more complex work scopes, and still deliver on time

- The role of **governments** in setting local content policy and regulations that encourage companies to utilise and develop the capability of local suppliers, but to do so in ways that leave room for innovation and build local suppliers capable of winning future work on a truly internationally competitive basis

- How **metrics for measuring and reporting of local content** need to be chosen and interpreted with care (see Box 4.1 and Chapter 9)

Plate 4.3 **Installation of Poinsettia platform deck onto jacket**

# A footnote

In December 2009, BG Trinidad and Tobago's Poinsettia project won the prestigious Overseas Project of the Year Award from the UK-based Association of Project Management (APM). Feedback from the judging panel was that delivering a project on schedule and within budget, while important, does not make a project exceptional. According to the judges, this project demonstrated BG T&T's empowerment of the local industry to take on the challenge of building a 4,300 tonne gas platform, which was far larger than anything they had undertaken before in Trinidad, utilising local subcontractors with zero lost-time incidents.

# 5

# Major contract tenders

## Factoring local content into the formulation of invitations to tender and tender evaluation for major contracts

For the effective management of local content, first-tier service contractors and suppliers play an important role. For example, it is common for the client company of a major project—such as power plant, highway or LNG facility—involving proven engineering, to grant responsibility for the procurement of goods and services to a handful of main contractors (sometimes a single contractor). These contractors usually have international experience, access to global supply chains and can leverage their size to secure cost advantages. Design-and-build and EPC/EPCm/EPIC contracts typically govern the contractual arrangements for this type of procurement, with client oversight being either light, in the case of lump-sum contracts, or substantial: for example, contracts based on project partnering principles or where compensation is dominated by unit rates.

In the operation and maintenance of major facilities and infrastructure, the extent to which the client devolves responsibility for procurement is more likely to vary. In some cases the client may have an in-house contracts department which exerts direct control over the majority of procurement. At the other end of the spectrum, the client may elect to outsource the entire operation of a plant or facility (not uncommon in the power generation sector). Alternatively, the client may parcel procurement into a series of individual long-term contracts—three to five years, with extensions awarded on performance—with responsibility for managing lower-tier supply chains passed to the contractor. Facilities management contracts and equipment leasing and maintenance contracts fall into this category.

To illustrate the importance of major contracts in local content management: in one typical large-scale capital project for an international integrated energy company[1] 81% of the total value of expenditure on goods and services was procured through seven lead contractors; and in another example, 69% of procurement expenditure through eight lead contractors.

It is the formulation of tender documents and tender evaluation criteria for high-value and long-term contracts that is the subject of this chapter. The central proposition is that, for major construction and operations contracts, the formulation of invitations to tender (ITTs) and tender evaluation criteria, and the choice of the basis for contract award, offer considerable scope to incentivise first-tier contractors to play a pivotal role in hiring and training national workers, local sourcing and local supplier development.

Given that such large proportions of capital and operational expenditure can be procured through such a small number of major contracts, it is perhaps surprising that clients and regulators have not made more use of the associated tendering processes to support their policies and strategies on local content. Instead, clients have tended to focus on the procurement process primarily with a mind to meeting minimal concession and regulatory compliance requirements for local content, while relying on philanthropic (social investment) projects and programmes to develop local suppliers (for

---

1 M. Warner, 'Building International Competitiveness of Domestic Suppliers: Policy and Experience in BG Group', presentation at the *5th Global Summit on Local Content*, London, 30 September 2009.

example, through dedicated SME technical and business management training, and, on occasions, access to finance).[2]

Likewise, state regulators rarely require the basis for contract award
to be more sophisticated than to satisfy minimum policy targets for
local content, or to grant domestic suppliers a price advantage.

## Purpose of the chapter

This chapter proposes enhancements to the tendering process to support delivery of a client or government's local content strategy or policy. The enhancements are applicable to contested tenders for major
capital project contracts and operations and maintenance contracts:
that is, contracts in which a substantial part of the contract value is
to be managed by the winning contractor to procure goods and services from subcontractors and suppliers, either domestic or foreign.

The focus is on enhancing invitations to tender (ITTs) and tender
evaluation criteria for major contracts, rather than ITTs and requests
for quotes (RFQs) or requests for proposals (RFPs) for minor purchase agreements and service contracts. The chapter offers guidance
in the following areas of ITT formulation and tender evaluation:

- Options for integrating local content considerations within
  the **basis of contract award** (technical vs. commercial, use
  of a K-factor)

- Whether to adopt dedicated **instructions to tenderers** on
  local content in the ITT or integrate questions on local content within existing instructions, e.g. on subcontractors

- How to include local content considerations in **tender evaluation plans** (scoring, weightings, mandatory thresholds)

- Formulation of pro forma **contract provisions** (articles of
  agreement) for local content

---

2  See, for example, the 'Zimele' risk finance facility managed by Anglo
   American.

## Local content and contract award

The first consideration in making enhancements to tender proce-dures to accommodate local content is to decide on what basis local content (local employment and skills development, local sourcing and local supplier development) will impact contract award. A key decision is whether local content is to be a factor in the tenderer's technical or commercial submission.

Commonly contracts are awarded either on the basis of lowest price (assuming satisfaction of technical requirements), or on the basis of the 'most economically advantageous tender'. Applying 'low-est technically acceptable price' carries an obvious disadvantage with regard to local content. Where the tenderer proposes a high-quality programme of local recruitment and training, combined with maxi-mum local sourcing and targeted supplier support and development, this will likely cost the client more than a low-quality offer, where the tenderer might propose little more than to train its national staff in health and safety. Inviting a tenderer to make a high-quality offer on local content carries the risk of reducing its price competitiveness. There are essentially three ways to manage this perverse impact, as follows:

The first option is to establish clear, quantified requirements for what the tender is being asked to deliver on local content, and require all tenderers to achieve the same level of performance. One way to do this is to expand the list of minimum technical requirements on local content (e.g. using mandatory pass/fail thresholds), similar to the way in which tenderers are obliged to meet health, safety and environmental minimum standards. So, for example, the technical requirements in the tender document may ask for a description and quantification of how a pre-set number of hours of training will be conducted for national workers; or a commitment to pre-established targets for sourcing from domestic suppliers: for example, suppliers of certain categories of goods or services, or suppliers geographically proximate to a project or operation, or suppliers owned by disadvan-taged or indigenous groups.

However, locking down expectations on local content in this way carries some clear disadvantages. For example, with regard to supporting domestic suppliers to develop their capabilities and competitiveness during contract execution (sometimes a priority of the host government), it is difficult to pre-establish what level of support the winning contractor should give. Different tenderers will have different prior relationships with local suppliers, and if the contract includes the finalisation of engineering design, the tenderer may not yet know precisely what services or goods it will need to procure.

More importantly perhaps, stipulating the expected quality of local content prior to tendering can be considered a wasted opportunity for soliciting innovation from tenderers. Given the considerable experience many international and large domestic contractors have in developing the capability and competitiveness of local supply chains, the process of competitive tendering is an opportunity to apply this experience to gain competitive advantage. If the expectations on local content are already fully codified in the scope of work and articles of agreement, then the only area left for competition is price.

A second option is to implicitly recognise that what constitutes a high-quality offer on local content is uncertain, and so instead treat this part of the bid as provisional. There are a number of ways to do this within the tender documents, as follows:

- Provide tenderers with a **ring-fenced budget**, and invite their proposals for a comprehensive local content development plan that most cost-effectively utilises this sum, framed either by performance expectations (e.g. percentage of nationals trained in particular skills such as welding, or subcontractors of named services brought up to ISO 14001, ISO 9001 and OHSAS 19001 standards by end of contract period), or by generalised headings (e.g. training of nationals; local sourcing; facilitation of joint ventures)

- Invite tenderers to provide a comprehensive local content development plan, but **separate the price** of the plan from the final bid price. In this case the quality of the plan continues to be assessed as part of bid evaluation, with the price component left optional. Once a preferred bidder is identified (based on lowest technically acceptable price), the client can enter pre-award negotiations with the bidder to decide whether to include the plan, or certain best parts of it, within the scope of work. This approach makes two important assumptions: (i) that the client's estimated contract price accommodates such a budget line; and (ii) that the applicable procurement rules allow clients to negotiate with bidders on price post the opening of tenders

- Invite tenderers to submit a comprehensive local content development plan as an entirely **alternative proposal**. This proposal does not form part of the formal tender evaluation, but the client would be entitled to include all or parts of the proposal in the scope of work, either as a negotiated lump sum or on a cost plus basis, or some combination

A third option is to decide to award the contract on the basis of what is most economically advantageous: that is, to bring together within a single award formula the quality and price of the tenderer's offer on local content.

One method is to take the variance in technical scores on local content between the tenderers (where the tenderer with the highest score sets the baseline) and apply this variance to the tenderer's estimated contract price (this will be a combination of the fixed bid priced elements plus estimates against the tendered unit rates). Then a corrective K-factor is applied to generate an overall technical value that reflects this original variance. This technical variance value is then added to the estimated contract price to give an overall integrated contract value.

Figure 5.1 demonstrates how a K-factor might be applied to the local content components of a technical submission (in this example a K-factor is not applied to the technical score for health and safety, which is assumed to require a mandatory minimum pass of 35, i.e. all three bidders have passed minimum health and safety requirements). A key advantage of applying a K-factor to local content and communicating this to all tenderers prior to tender submission, is to reduce the disincentive faced by tenderers on price competitiveness when proposing a high-quality submission on local content.

In summary then, the first option—incorporating precise expectations on local content into the technical submission—levels the playing field between tenderers on price, but risks stifling innovation by the bidding contractors (this is an important consideration because it is a well-informed lead contractor, and not the client, who is often best placed to understand what is possible with regard to local employment and the supplier market).

The second option—of treating the tenderer's proposals on local content as provisional (through a ring-fenced budget, separated pricing or alternative proposal)—removes the disincentive on price competitiveness of the first option, but carries a potentially higher overall cost to the client.

The third option—applying a K-factor—introduces the discipline of 'cost-effectiveness' by bringing together the quality and price of the tenderer's proposals on local content. There is however a risk here that the choice of K-factor is open to manipulation to give advantage to (or temper the impact on) particular bidders; for example, regulators using a K-factor to preference domestic contractors over foreign contractors.

## Figure 5.1 **Illustration of K-factor on bid price**

|  | Score | Max |
|---|---|---|
| **Technical submission of tenderer A** | | |
| **Health and safety** | 40 | 50 |
| *Local content* | | |
| Employment of nationals | 5 | 10 |
| Training for nationals | 5 | 10 |
| Communication of local supplier opportunities | 5 | 10 |
| Support to domestic suppliers | 10 | 10 |
| Local content as % of contract value | 5 | 10 |
| *Total technical score (as %)* | **70** | 100 |
| *Estimated contract price of tenderer A* | | **$220** |
| *Technical score variance (max tech−A tech, as % of max tech)* | | **9.1%** |

| | Score | Max |
|---|---|---|
| **Technical submission of tenderer B** | | |
| **Health and safety** | 42 | 50 |
| *Local content* | | |
| Employment of nationals | 7 | 10 |
| Training for nationals | 7 | 10 |
| Communication of local supplier opportunities | 6 | 10 |
| Support to domestic suppliers | 9 | 10 |
| Local content as % of contract value | 6 | 10 |
| *Total technical score (as %)* | **77** | 100 |
| *Estimated contract price of tenderer B* | | **$230** |
| *Technical score variance (max tech−B tech, as % of max tech)* | | **0.0%** |

| | Score | Max |
|---|---|---|
| **Technical submission of tenderer C** | | |
| **Health and safety** | 38 | 50 |
| *Local content* | | |
| Employment of nationals | 4 | 10 |
| Training for nationals | 4 | 10 |
| Communication of local supplier opportunities | 3 | 10 |
| Support to domestic suppliers | 8 | 10 |
| Local content as % of contract value | 2 | 10 |
| *Total technical score (as %)* | **59** | 100 |
| *Estimated contract price of tenderer C* | | **$210** |
| *Technical score variance (max tech−C tech, as % of max tech)* | | **23.4%** |

| **Application of K-factor (0.65)** | | |
|---|---|---|
| *Estimated contract price* | *Technical variance value* | *Integrated contract value* |
| A | $220 | $13.0 | $233.0 |
| B | $230 | $0.0 | **$230.0** |
| C | **$210** | $31.9 | $241.9 |

# Instructions to tenderers: a dedicated or integrated questionnaire?

When providing instructions to tenderers on what information to submit on local content, should these instructions form a dedicated questionnaire or 'schedule' on local content, or should such questions be integrated within existing instructions?

If adopting an integrated approach, the most obvious candidates for adaptation to the existing instructions are:

- Infrastructure and plant

- Human resources

- Subcontracting

- Risk management

A disadvantage of adapting the existing common suite of instructions is that this may lead to muddled responses. Many such instructions are model questions, and tenderers have standardised policies and codes they use to provide responses. Tenderers may also have personnel dedicated to answering each type of questionnaire and draw on performance or market data readily accessible within their company. Adding one or two additional questions on local content to such standardised tender questions may cause confusion. In addition, there are certain questions on local content that do not readily fall under existing questionnaires. Further, without a dedicated set of instructions on local content the message that this aspect is to play a significant part in tender evaluation may be lost.

Assuming that a dedicated set of instructions on local content is beneficial for the reasons cited above, its principal disadvantage is the risk of repetition. For example, asking a tenderer for information on its infrastructure in-country, proposals for the training of nationals, and how it intends to communicate subcontracting opportunities to domestic suppliers, could appear repetitious when the tenderer is concurrently asked to provide details of its operational infrastructure in a questionnaire on infrastructure, of training on health and safety in an HSE questionnaire, and of its subcontracting practices in a questionnaire on subcontracting.

More worrying perhaps, such duplication runs the risk of inadvertent double-counting on price: for example, on training costs.

On balance, though, if the client wishes to communicate to tenderers the seriousness with which proposals on local content will contribute towards contract award, and such instructions on local content within ITTs are relatively new for the client or contractor, then providing a dedicated local content schedule is well advised.

The more complicated this local content questionnaire, the more important it will be to offer guidance to the tenderer in how to respond. This may include not only additional guidance and examples with the document itself, but orientation meetings with those on the bid list.

The next section provides advice on preparing a dedicated set of instructions to tenderers on local content.

## Preparing local content instructions to tenderers

The range of local content requirements and activities that might be included in dedicated instructions to tenderer (or 'Schedule') is well documented.[3] In the first instance, consideration needs to be given to legal, regulatory and contractual requirements on local content, including reporting obligations (see Box 5.1).

Beyond transposing the applicable compliance requirements on local content within instructions to tenderers, the client may elect to solicit additional proposals on local content that are not mandated but form part of its strategy. A selection of these is given in Box 5.2.

---

3 See, for example, ODI, *Extractive Industries and Local Economic Development: Incentivising Innovation by Lead Contractors through Contract Tendering* (London: Overseas Development Institute, 2004).

Box 5.1 **Examples of requirements on local content for inclusion in instructions to tenderers**

---

Hiring and training of nationals

- Minimum number or proportion of national workers involved in contract execution (sometimes disaggregated by skill or management level of worker)
- Minimum training provided to national workers, either by absolute monetary value, proportion of contract value, or number of training hours (total or per person)
- Obligations arising from environmental and social impact assessment studies required as part of statutory approvals, e.g. on employment or training of persons from project-affected communities or specified indigenous peoples

Local sourcing

- Information on capabilities of domestic supplier market
- Requirements to disclose procurement opportunities to domestic supplier market
- Preference in the acquisition of goods and services from domestic suppliers (provided they are offered on competitive terms and conditions)
- Price advantage to domestic suppliers if able to meet technical requirements, e.g. 10%
- Minimum targets for percentage of contract value to be procured from domestic suppliers located in the host country or owned by nationals, or sourced as goods and services of domestic origin
- Obligations on local sourcing arising from environmental and social impact assessment studies required as part of statutory approvals (e.g. obligations to use suppliers owned by indigenous groups or based in project-affected communities)

Reporting requirements

- Reporting on performance against the above compliance requirements
- Additional reporting on local content that is not necessarily a legal obligation but committed to by the client, e.g. GRI reporting on economic impacts[a]

a   Global Reporting Initiative on corporate reporting of governance, environmental and social indicators.

---

## Box 5.2 Proposals on local content beyond compliance, for instructions to tenderers

### Tenderer's capabilities

- Tenderer's general capabilities and infrastructure in the host country
- Tenderer's capabilities and infrastructure relevant to contract execution
- New capital investments to be brought into the host country to execute the contract
- New alliances, partnerships and joint ventures with national firms to execute contract and transfer technology

### Hiring and training

- Outreach activities and procedures for maximising the direct hiring of nationals
- National worker development programme linked to gaps in local skills that carry risks to contract performance
- Anticipated levels of national workers in subcontracts
- Proposals for demobilisation of national workers and retrenchment to alternative employment

### Local sourcing

- Classification of subcontracts and supplier opportunities based on domestic capability, risks to contract performance and opportunities to align with government priorities for industrial competitiveness and economic diversification
- Outreach support to domestic suppliers to access procurement opportunities, e.g. pre-qualification, navigation of tendering process

### Supplier development and competitiveness

- Support for domestic suppliers and subcontractors to deliver contract performance
- Support for specific domestic suppliers and subcontractors to expand and market their business post contract completion, e.g. those industrial categories that present long-term cost saving to the client, or are of high importance to national, regional or local economic development, or offer compensation to communities adversely affected by a project

### Public access to operational infrastructure

- Expectations for public access to operational infrastructure, e.g. transport, utilities

# Principles for structuring instructions to tenderers on local content

The process of formulating dedicated instructions to tenderers on local content should follow certain principles, as follows:

- In the opening 'General Instructions':
  - Give guidance as to the relative importance the client is intending to place on local content compared with other parts of the tender
  - Draw attention to the need to quantify proposals and complete template tables, as appropriate
  - Where relevant, provide clarity that the proposals may be directly included as contract provisions

- Instructions to tenderers should broadly reflect subsequent tender evaluation criteria, and not leave the tenderer guessing as to which parts of their submission on local content carry the most weight

- If asking tenderers to provide information not usually solicited in conventional tenders (which can be the majority of questions on local content, especially those in Box 5.2), provide examples and additional guidance within the instructions, and, as noted, if necessary convene orientation meetings with tenderers to clarify expectations

- If soliciting qualitative information (e.g. descriptions of training programmes for nationals or programmes of support for domestic suppliers) subdivide these instructions and clearly itemise. This will reduce subjectivity in the subsequent evaluation process, and enable more targeted follow-up clarification questions should tenderers omit certain information

- Where possible, ask for the quantification of the tenderers proposals and provide the expected parameters (for example, as tabulated templates). This reduces the use of different metrics by different tenderers (for example, the training of nationals by one tenderer being quantified as 'average training hours per national worker', and by another tenderer as

'total training hours across contract period'. Further, providing the metrics forms the basis for establishing subsequent
milestones and targets against which contract performance
can be measured and contract payments made

- Invite tenderers to bring their proposals on different aspects
  of local content into a single document: for example, a local
  content development plan

# Tender evaluation of local content

As with conventional tender evaluation, there are essentially four
considerations in the formulation of criteria to evaluate responses to
instructions on local content.

First is the **range of scores**—usually zero to three or zero to five.
'One' can be omitted, so that the range is 0–2–3–4–5. A score of 0
(not 1) should be assigned in cases where the tenderer has failed to
submit any information. (Note that failure to submit the requested
information may require the evaluator to clarify with the tenderer
whether the omission is intentional, especially if the questions are
unfamiliar to the tenderer.)

Second, is the **relative weighting** to be given to each item being
evaluated. For example, the client may wish to weight the entire section on local content on a par with that for health, safety and environment (HSE), or may consider local content to be less important
and weight accordingly.

Within the suite of questions being evaluated, the client may wish
to give more or less importance to certain questions, such as investment in technology transfer, or the anticipated proportion of goods
of domestic origin. This logic applies equally to sub-questions within
one category of local content: for example, to the hiring of nationals
from the region where a project is located, compared with hiring of
nationals from other regions.

Third is to consider whether there should be **mandatory thresholds**, below which the tenderer is considered to have failed, and thus
is not eligible for consideration for award. For example, if the basis

of contract award is to be 'technically acceptable, lowest price', then some threshold for overall lowest acceptable score on the technical submission may be needed; 60% is not uncommon. However, such a generalised threshold may pass tenderers on their technical submission even if they have low scores in areas of contract performance considered important to the successful execution of the contract, which increasingly includes local content. (It is for this reason that tender evaluation of different health, safety and environmental items are frequently subject to individual mandatory thresholds.)

Mandatory thresholds for local content are most likely for responses to questions in the following areas:

- Legal and contractual **obligations** on the client for hiring and local sourcing, e.g. a minimum score of 3 (out of 5) assigned to the minimum obligation, and scores of 4 and 5 assigned if the tenderer exceeds the minimum

- Training for national workers and support for domestic suppliers in those particular categories of skills or goods/services that carry particular **risk** for the client if not performed or delivered to requirements

- Support for domestic suppliers to expand their business in goods and services most closely aligned with either: (i) the **client's needs** for long-term cost savings; or (ii) **government priorities** for industrial competitiveness or economic diversification

Table 5.1 provides an example of how scoring, weighting and mandatory thresholds might be applied to a tenderer's tender submission on local content. *Table 5.1 is an illustration only.*

A fourth consideration is the **choice of tender evaluation criteria**, whether quantitative or qualitative. For each normative scale (0 to 5, or 1 to 5) the criteria applicable to a score of 5 should be such that not all tenderers would be expected to reach that level. To this end, key questions to frame formulation of the criteria are: (i) what does a poor response look like? (ii) What is likely to be a just adequate or satisfactory response (including mandatory thresholds if applicable)? (iii) What does excellence look like?

For quantitative criteria, these need to match the metrics used in the instructions to tenderers. Likewise, for qualitative criteria, these should largely be based on the language and examples used to inform the tenderer to prepare their submission. They should not introduce new concepts.

A common practice in the formulation of qualitative criteria is to list the range of expectations that, in combination, would constitute a score of 5; then refer in the criteria for lower scores to a subset of these items. An example might be to assign a score of 3 for submissions that cover three of six requested items, or two if one of these is described in particular detail.

Table 5.1 **Illustration of scoring, weighting and mandatory thresholds in evaluation of tender submissions on local content**

| | Instructions to tenderer | Mandatory thresholds | Score (0, 2, 3, 4, 5) | Weightings | Weight adjusted |
|---|---|---|---|---|---|
| 1 | **Health and safety** | | | **40.0%** | 28.6% |
| 2 | **Quality management** | | | **10.0%** | 6.2% |
| 3 | **Contractor experience** | | | **10.0%** | 5.9% |
| 4 | **Local content** | | | **40.0%** | 23.6% |
| 4.1 | **Tenderer's capabilities in-country** | | | 10.0% | |
| 4.1a | Prior investment over last three years in country relevant to contract performance | 0 | | 3.0% | 0.0% |
| 4.1b | Capital investment in country if awarded contract | 2 | | 3.0% | 1.2% |
| 4.1c | Proposals for joint ventures or alliances with national contractors | 3 | | 4.0% | 2.4% |
| 4.2 | **National labour in contract execution** | | | 4.0% | |
| 4.2a | National workers in management positions | 1 | | 2.0% | 0.4% |

| | Instructions to tenderer | Mandatory thresholds | Score (0, 2, 3, 4, 5) | Weightings | Weight adjusted |
|---|---|---|---|---|---|
| 4.2b | Total national workers utilised in contract | 3 | 3 | 2.0% | 1.2% |
| 4.3 | **Training of national labour** | | | 4.0% | |
| 4.3a | Average training hours per national worker | | 4 | 2.0% | 1.6% |
| 4.3b | Average training hours in skill shortage areas critical to contract | 3 | 5 | 2.0% | 2.0% |
| 4.4 | **Local sourcing** | | | 8.0% | |
| 4.4a | Communication of procurement opportunities to domestic suppliers, including navigation of tendering procedures | 3 | 3 | 3.0% | 1.8% |
| 4.4b | Proportion of contract value on goods and services of domestic origin | 3 | 3 | 5.0% | 3.0% |
| 4.5 | **Domestic suppliers development and competitiveness** | | | 11.0% | |
| 4.5a | Support for suppliers and subcontractors to execute contract | 3 | 4 | 6.0% | 4.8% |
| 4.5b | Support for suppliers and subcontractors to improve competitiveness and align with technology transfer priorities of government | | 4 | 5.0% | 4.0% |
| 4.6 | **Operational infrastructure for public use** | | | 3.0% | |
| 4.6a | Proposals for public access to operational infrastructure, e.g. transport, utilities | | 2 | 3.0% | 1.2% |
| | | | Total weighted score | | 64.3% |
| | | | Minimum pass | | 60.0% |

# Pro forma contract provisions for local content

It is convention to include the principal articles of agreement that the winning tenderer will be obliged to meet in invitations to tenderers as model contract provisions, along with further provisions in dedicated pro forma exhibits: for example, administrative procedures exhibit, HSE exhibit.

If an ITT has included a dedicated set of instructions to tenderers on local content, it is logical to include a corresponding contract exhibit on local content. First and foremost this exhibit will include the compliance requirements that the client is obliged to pass to the contractor in order to comply with its own legal and regulatory commitments. This might include, for example, training of nationals or minimum proportion of contract value spent on goods and services of domestic origin.

Regarding the tenderer's proposals on local content that go beyond these minimum requirements, the client essentially has three options in formulating a local content exhibit, as follows:

- **Option 1**. Simply carry the tenderer's proposals through to the contract as **unaltered obligations**. This requires the local content exhibit to be little more than a 'place holder' for the details of the winning tenderer's proposal. The disadvantage of this approach is that the winning proposals on local content may not be sufficiently developed to be contractually binding or to provide for performance reporting. There may be omissions in the required responses, or some responses may be unsatisfactory to the client but against which there was no mandatory threshold in the tender evaluation

- **Option 2**. The pro forma exhibit provides the **main headings** and some limited information on what is expected, similar to the headings and supporting text in columns 1 and 2 of Table 5.1. The advantage of this approach is that it reinforces to the tenderer the importance of providing responses to all the instructions in the local content schedule. Further, if the winning bid still has omissions, the exhibit can be used to guide the pre-award negotiations so that gaps are filled

- **Option 3**. **Fully codify** in the scope of work and exhibit what the contractor will be expected to deliver on all aspects of local content, both the transposed compliance requirements and activities that go beyond compliance. This approach reduces, and potentially negates, the need for dedicated instructions to tenderers on local content. It also levels the playing field on the pricing of local content (see discussion earlier). A disadvantage is that it may stifle innovation and reduce competition between tenderers on local content. It also assumes that the client fully understands what the local skill gaps are, the training needs of nationals, what levels of local sourcing are possible and how suppliers and sub-contractors might best be supported during contract execution—knowledge more likely than not to be in the hands of major contractors rather than the client

Two other key considerations in formulating a local content exhibit are payment arrangements and reporting requirements.

Whether incorporated directly in the local content exhibit, or cross-referenced to the compensation provisions in the main pro forma contract, a decision is needed on how performance by the contractor in meetings its obligations on local content will be tied to compensation payments. The obvious consideration in making this decision is to be clear what the implications for the contract and commercial and reputational interest of the client are should the obligations on local content not be met. Referencing back to the overarching procurement strategy for the project (Chapter 3) should be helpful. For example, will poor performance on local content by the main contractor lead to material costs or risks, such as fines or rejection of cost recovery claims if local content targets are missed; or delays to the project schedule or risks to operational quality if the contractor's support to local suppliers fails to ensure contract execution to international standards.

It is more likely that those aspects of a tenderer's proposal on local content that carry such material commercial risks and costs (or form part of the reputation of the company with government or other stakeholders) would need to be tied directly to compensation payments. In contrast, where the risks and costs are manageable or low, it may make more sense to bring compensation for these activities under the umbrella of other similar lower-risk activities and make payments against broader milestones of contract delivery.

In either case, the pro forma local content exhibit will need to clarify (either directly or by citing the relevant compensation provisions) the consequences for non-conformance.

Regardless of whether the local content exhibit is based on 'dropping in' the tenderer's proposals or provides specific headings and guidance, the exhibit will need to codify the client's expectations for reporting on local content performance. The reporting metrics to be used will largely be taken from the quantitative information tenderers are asked to provide in their bids: for example, on training, local sourcing or supplier development. But there may be additional reporting that the client wishes to include: for example, on how contract execution has improved local supplier competitiveness, such as labour productivity, service delivery and product quality, or metrics that the client's parent company needs to prepare its annual sustainability report.

Finally, there is the question of how to handle incomplete proposals on local content. Unless all expectations on local content are fully mandated (either through minimum thresholds in tender evaluation or through explicit expectations in the scope of work and contract provisions), it is likely that the proposal on local content of the winning tender will not be complete. There are three main ways to handle this challenge:

- Use the period of negotiation with the preferred bidder to finalise the proposal (this may be unrealistic given the time available and/or regulatory prohibition on pre-award negotiations on price)

- Use this same period to mature the proposal, but sufficient only to clarify the price of the proposals, any capital investment and alliance commitments by the contractor, and the reporting and compensation arrangements including milestones; but allowing the contractor to finalise further details in a defined period post contract award: for example, 30 days (this is more manageable than the first option, yet ensures that the tenderer's formulation of an offer on local content still coincides with the client's maximum period of influence)

- Agree a provisional sum, then allow the winning contractor a defined period after contract award to finalise proposals (this is potentially more palatable to the contractor, but may reduce the client's leverage to solicit the best deal on local content)

## Conclusions

Table 5.2 summarises key decisions that need to be taken when incorporating local content into invitations to tender and tender evaluation criteria for major contracts. The main options, and their advantages and disadvantages, have been discussed in this chapter. In taking the right decisions, due consideration should be given to the importance placed on local content in the relevant procurement strategy (see Chapter 3). In addition, professional advice must be sought from contract managers with oversight of the entire tendering process, as well as legal advice on the proposed contract provisions and applicable competition and anti-discrimination law.

## Table 5.2 Key decisions for incorporating local content within ITTs and tender evaluation criteria for major contracts

### Key decisions

#### Basis of contract award

1. Should local content proposals be solicited from tenderers as part of their technical or commercial submissions?
2. How to mange the effect of high-quality local content proposals on the tenderer's price competitiveness (codification, provisional sums, K-factor, etc.)

#### Instructions to tenderers

3. Should instructions to tenderer on local content be integrated within other questionnaires (e.g. resource planning or subcontracting), or separated as a dedicated local content schedule?
4. How to transform local content legal and regulatory compliance requirements on the client into instructions to tender
5. How far should instructions to tenders go beyond compliance requirements, e.g. for reasons of risk management, long-term cost saving, or reputation differentiation?
6. What principles apply in the formulation of instructions to tenderer on local content, including linking questions to subsequent tender evaluation criteria, quantitative vs. qualitative questions, ad hoc responses vs. combined local content development plan

#### Tender evaluation

7. What relative weightings to assign to different topics on local content, e.g. meeting local content targets vs. support to domestic suppliers
8. Should mandatory threshold be introduced to certain local content topics?

#### Pro forma contract provisions

9. Should pro forma contract provisions in the ITT be: (i) place-holder; (ii) headings with guidance; or (iii) codified contractual obligations?
10. Are local content considerations sufficiently material to the client to warrant linking compensation payments to contractor's local content performance?
11. If linked, should compensation be combined with performance in other areas of the scope of work, or restricted to local content?
12. What sanctions should apply for non-conformance or under-performance by the contractor on its local content obligations?
13. What reporting metrics should be included as contractual obligations?
14. What to do if the quality of the winning contractor's proposals on local content is insufficient to be incorporated as contractual obligations

# 6

# Accessible procurement

## Designing procurement procedures to facilitate access for local suppliers

Different definitions of small- and medium-scale enterprises (SMEs) abound, from unregulated micro firms in the informal sector, to what in poorer economies would constitute large companies employing hundreds of people. In this book we adhere to the definitions adopted by the World Bank Group. The International Finance Corporation, the private sector arm of the World Bank Group, defines SMEs as follows:[1]

---

1 International Finance Corporation, 'Creating Opportunities for Small Business', 2008; www.ifc.org/ifcext/sme.nsf/AttachmentsByTitle/ ifcandsmes_brochure2007/$FILE/IFCandSMEs_Brochure2007.pdf, accessed 15 June 2011. International Finance Corporation, 'Build Your Business Tool Kit'; www.smetoolkit.org/smetoolkit/en, accessed 15 June 2011.

- **Small enterprises**. 10 to 50 people, with total assets and/ or sales between US$100,000 and US$3 million, and with financing needs of loan size US$10,000 to US$100,000

- **Medium enterprises**. 50 to 300 people, with total assets and/ or sales between US$3 million and US$15 million, and with finance needs of loan size US$100,000 to US$1–2 million

For governments, whether in developed or developing countries, the SME sector is often viewed as a key driver for employment creation and technology innovation. That said, the common assertion that SMEs are the *primary* engine of growth and employment can be exaggerated. The Organisation for Economic Co-operation and Development (OECD) draws an important distinction between the SME sector as a whole and those that exhibit high potential for growth, the so-called 'gazelle' SMEs.

In high-income countries, for the SME sector as a whole, OECD research concludes that job creation averages 5% per year.[2] This is a gross figure. In reality, job turnover in the SME sector is high and many new-starts fail in their first few years. The same OECD research found that net job creation in SMEs was actually 1%. Similar research could not be found to be able to give comparable figures for middle- or low-income countries. What is evident, however, is that the SME sector takes a smaller share of a country's total formal employment the less economically advanced the country. For example, in low-income countries the share of SMEs in formal employment is around 17%, compared with 60% in high-income countries.[3]

This pattern is repeated with the contribution of SMEs to a country's GDP; 16% is contributed by SMEs in low-income countries, compared with 51% in high-income countries. As noted in a recent United Nations report: 'the reality in many poor countries . . . is that the small and medium enterprise sector is relatively marginal in the

---

2 Organisation for Economic Co-operation and Development, *High Growth SMEs and Employment* (Geneva: OECD, 2002; www.oecd.org/dataoecd/18/28/2493092.pdf).

3 UNDP, *Unleashing Entrepreneurship: Making Business Work for the Poor* (New York: United Nations Development Programme, Commission on the Private Sector and Development, 2004; www.undp.org/cpsd/documents/report/english/fullreport.pdf).

domestic ecosystem . . . [unable] to graduate to the ranks of larger companies'.[4]

# Common constraints on SMEs

The constraints to SMEs taking a larger share of employment and the economy in poorer economies are many. These include, *inter alia*:

- **State bureaucratic barriers** to entry for new firms, e.g. length of time and number of separate procedural steps involved in registering a business to operate or for tax purposes; set-up costs, including facilitation payments

- **Corporate bureaucratic barriers** to entry, e.g. procurement pre-qualification hurdles biased towards long-standing established firms; international quality and health and safety standards

- **High cost of accessing credit**, due, for example, to a lack of equity and accumulated assets, poor visibility by financial institutions of the creditworthiness of SME owners, inflexible risk assessment criteria of local lenders that over-prices SME risk

- **Regulatory compliance costs**, including fees for meeting legal and tax obligations, health, safety and environmental standards and reporting obligations, and, more recently, requirements to report on local content and assure ethical conduct (e.g. maintain risk register)

- **Tax laws** that financially penalise smaller firms disproportionately compared with larger firms

- **Lower labour productivity** due to older technology and lower-waged skills

page 132 ➜

---

4 *Ibid*: 13.

Table 6.1  Ranking of a sample of mineral-producing countries by ease of doing business

| Economy | Overall ease of doing business rank | Starting a business | | | | Getting credit | | |
|---|---|---|---|---|---|---|---|---|
| | | Rank | Procedures (number) | Time (days) | Cost (% of income per capita) | Rank | Strength of legal rights index (0–10) | Depth of credit information index (0–6) |
| South Africa | 34 | 75 | 6 | 22 | 6 | 2 | 9 | 6 |
| Peru | 36 | 54 | 6 | 27 | 13.6 | 15 | 7 | 6 |
| Chile | 43 | 62 | 8 | 22 | 6.8 | 72 | 4 | 5 |
| Botswana | 52 | 90 | 10 | 61 | 2.2 | 46 | 7 | 4 |
| Ghana | 67 | 99 | 7 | 12 | 20.3 | 46 | 8 | 3 |
| Namibia | 69 | 124 | 10 | 66 | 18.5 | 15 | 8 | 5 |
| Zambia | 76 | 57 | 6 | 18 | 27.9 | 6 | 9 | 5 |
| Jamaica | 81 | 18 | 6 | 8 | 5.2 | 89 | 8 | 0 |
| Papua New Guinea | 103 | 81 | 6 | 51 | 17.7 | 89 | 5 | 3 |
| Sierra Leone | 143 | 61 | 6 | 12 | 110.7 | 128 | 6 | 0 |
| Ukraine | 145 | 118 | 10 | 27 | 6.1 | 32 | 9 | 3 |
| Niger | 173 | 159 | 9 | 17 | 118.6 | 152 | 3 | 1 |
| Guinea | 179 | 181 | 13 | 41 | 146.6 | 168 | 3 | 0 |

Table 6.2 Ranking of a sample of oil-producing/exploring countries by ease of doing business

| Economy | Ease of doing business rank | Starting a business | | | | Getting credit | | |
|---|---|---|---|---|---|---|---|---|
| | | Rank | Procedures (number) | Time (days) | Cost (% of income per capita) | Rank | Strength of legal rights index (0–10) | Depth of credit information index (0–6) |
| United Kingdom | 4 | 17 | 6 | 13 | 0.7 | 2 | 9 | 6 |
| Norway | 8 | 33 | 5 | 7 | 1.8 | 46 | 7 | 4 |
| Australia | 10 | 2 | 2 | 2 | 0.7 | 6 | 9 | 5 |
| Saudi Arabia | 11 | 13 | 4 | 5 | 7 | 46 | 5 | 6 |
| Azerbaijan | 54 | 15 | 6 | 8 | 3.1 | 46 | 6 | 5 |
| Kazakhstan | 59 | 47 | 6 | 19 | 1 | 72 | 4 | 5 |
| Ghana | 67 | 99 | 7 | 12 | 20.3 | 46 | 8 | 3 |
| Trinidad and Tobago | 97 | 74 | 9 | 43 | 0.8 | 32 | 8 | 4 |
| Uganda | 122 | 137 | 18 | 25 | 94.4 | 46 | 7 | 4 |
| Russian Federation | 123 | 108 | 9 | 30 | 3.6 | 89 | 3 | 5 |
| Nigeria | 137 | 110 | 8 | 31 | 78.9 | 89 | 8 | 0 |
| Timor-Leste | 174 | 167 | 10 | 83 | 18.4 | 182 | 1 | 0 |

- **Lack of or high cost of physical infrastructure** and utilities, including access to and affordability of clean water, energy, transportation, information technology

- The adverse influence and **market power** of larger suppliers

Tables 6.1 and 6.2 show the ranking of different mineral- and oil- and gas-producing economies with respect to the cost of SMEs going into business in these countries. Measures are given for two common indictors: the ease of starting a new business and securing credit.[5]

Noticeable is the relative time taken in many of these countries to overcome procedures to establishing a new business. For example, establishment takes, on average, 61 days in Botswana and 83 in Timor-Leste. This compares with 7 days in Norway and 13 days in the United Kingdom. Striking is that a number of middle- and low-income countries have succeeded in streamlining their bureaucracies for new-start SMEs, notably Azerbaijan (middle-income) down to 8 days, and Ghana (low-income) to 12 days.

In developing economies especially, a second critical barrier to SME participation in procurement is the market power influence of the larger, established suppliers. Across the oil, gas and mining sectors the influence of first-tier equipment and material suppliers and service contractor firms can be considerable. UNDP asserts that, in developing countries, 'large incumbent [first-tier] companies can stifle entrepreneurial energy and initiative . . . [taking] advantage of weak institutional environments to raise anticompetitive barriers and protect their dominant position'.[6] Although probably directed more towards private domestic and state-owned first-tier suppliers, this assertion can also apply to the foreign, multinational suppliers, since here the locked-in global sourcing arrangements and long-standing relationships with preferred sub-suppliers and sub-contractors can appear anticompetitive when viewed by domestic SMEs seeking to access the same procurement opportunities. (The role of market power in possibly justifying local content regulations is discussed in Chapter 1.)

---

5 World Bank, 'Doing Business', database; www.doingbusiness.org/
    Custom%20Query, accessed 15 June 2011.
6 UNDP, *Unleashing Entrepreneurship*: 14.

For further discussion on the different barriers to SME participation in the supply chains of private and public procurement opportunities, the reader is directed to the World Bank 'Doing Better Business' reports and website.[7]

## The importance of high-growth 'gazelle' SMEs

Given the numerous barriers to SME participation in large-scale procurement, and the evidence of a net negative contribution of SMEs to national employment, it is all the more important that for investments in oil, gas and mining developments to create sustainable jobs and grow the economy, SMEs need to be identified that have a high potential for growth. It is these high-growth SMEs that embody and nurture the entrepreneurial characteristics of successful economies. And, most crucially for public industrial and employment policy, it is high-growth SMEs that create the economic 'spillover effects' from inward investment that leads to sustainable employment and stimulates other new entrants into the local supply chains. 'Spillover effects' are the backward and forward economic linkages created by foreign and domestic investment. In the oil, gas and mining industries, they take place in two steps: first, as the creation or expansion of high-growth SMEs; second, these high-growth SMEs themselves give rise to other new entrants in their own value chain, either as backward linkages, for example, providing design, legal or insurance services or raw or processed materials, or forward linkages, for example, in the form of logistics and distribution services or equipment repair and maintenance services.

The challenge, then, for either industrial policy-makers or private procuring companies is first to identify who these high-growth SMEs are, and then provide them with appropriate support to unleash their full potential. Box 6.1 provides an inventory of indicators for identifying high-growth potential SMEs. The more of these indictors that can be found, the higher the likelihood that SMEs in this category

7 World Bank, 'Doing Business'.

for procurement will exhibit the potential for high growth, and with it bring sustainable employment and second-round backward and forward linkages.

## Box 6.1 Indicators of high-growth potential SMEs in the supply chains of oil, gas and mining development

- SMEs with successful performance record on previous contracts
- SMEs with higher than 50% annual growth rates over the last three years
- SMEs with a capability to access long-term and risk finance at affordable rates
- SMEs with strong and experienced leadership and management
- SMEs with a skilled workforce, paid at or above the market rate
- SMEs providing services or goods to a market that itself has strong growth potential
  - Includes markets with multiple buyers and buyers in synergistic sectors, e.g. construction
  - Includes markets supported by local content compliance regulations, e.g. domestic-only tender lists for certain commodities, local content targets for new sub-categories of procurement
  - Excludes markets based on one-off capital projects, such as a single offshore production unit
  - Excludes markets where barriers to entry are too high, e.g. excessive environmental standards, excessive credit ratings
  - Excludes markets that require prohibitively expensive licensing rights from OEMs (original equipment manufacturers)
- SMEs with a track record in winning contracts on their own merits on an internationally competitive basis (i.e. without collaboration or anticompetitive local preferencing), or at least are competitive in their home market across the main indicators of price, quality and delivery
- SMEs that have already won work in export markets
- SMEs that provide a range of products and services and are not dependent on a single client

## Strategies for SME participation

The discussion above points to two broad strategies for supporting the participation of local SMEs in supply chains within the oil, gas and mining sectors.

First is to identify and then nurture high-growth SMEs, that subset of SMEs likely to generate new employment, bring innovation, attract investment capital, cause spillover impacts across the economy, and be sustained and expand into the future. Such nurturing can take many forms, including programmes to facilitate access to affordable finance or financial guarantees, provide technical and management training, raise performance standards, or leveraging technology transfer and inward investment through joint ventures and alliances with established foreign and domestic firms. SME development programmes are explored in Chapter 7.

Second is to formulate corporate procurement processes and procedures to give fair opportunity to local SMEs to be able to access supply chains, either those procedures directly controlled by the investing company (or its operators) or those processes managed by first-tier suppliers who procure on behalf of their client. The role of procurement procedures in supporting or constraining the participation of high-growth local SMEs in the supply chains of oil, gas and mining companies is discussed below.

## Challenges to SME participation in procurement

An oil and gas or mining consortia involved in exploring or operating in a given country may have literally thousands of local SMEs registered with its procurement department. The hurdles to any one of these passing from vendor registration through to contract award are considerable. Figure 6.1 provides a schematic of some of these challenges. Each hurdle is discussed in turn below.

## Figure 6.1 **Challenges to local SME participation in the procurement process**

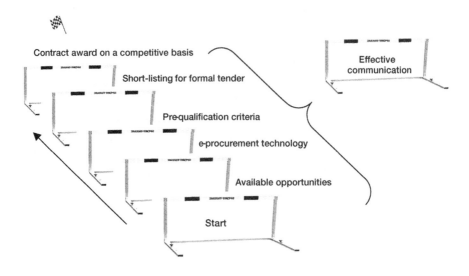

## Available opportunities

A commonly overlooked constraint to the participation of local SMEs in procurement by major companies or public procurement entities is the scope of the opportunity in the first place. This may be far smaller than the headline figure of planned expenditure might suggest. The limiting factors are fourfold.

First, the client may be operating highly specified equipment, requiring spare parts or service support of an equally technical nature, and/or only available from the original manufacturer or installation contractor. In other words, the budget for these particular goods or services may not generally be available, but require **sole sourcing**[8] (refer to Fig. 6.2).

8 **Sole sourcing**, defined as a no-bid contract where only one supplier can provide the contractual services or supply of goods needed, and any attempt to obtain bids would only result in one person or company being available to meet the need (Wikipedia; en.wikipedia.org/wiki/Sole_source, accessed 12 April 2011).

Second, for operations and repeat capital expenditure, the client may already be locked into long-term purchasing arrangements. Such agreements are negotiated with the intent of driving down costs or improving operational reliability, or both. Two- or three-year-long contracts, with options for one or two annual performance-based extensions are not uncommon. This further limits the availability of procurement opportunities.

Third, it is also not uncommon for contracts performed by larger suppliers, whether foreign or domestic, to be renewed rather than competitively re-tendered. A procuring company may be inclined to renew a contract in cases where, for example, the performance of the contractor in question has been of high quality and its service or delivery particularly reliable. (In other words, the contract is already in a safe pair of hands, so why change it?) Or, it might be that for the buyer the process of re-tendering is too time- or labour-intensive given pressures on schedule and human resourcing. To give some

Figure 6.2 **Common limitations on the availability of procurement opportunities**

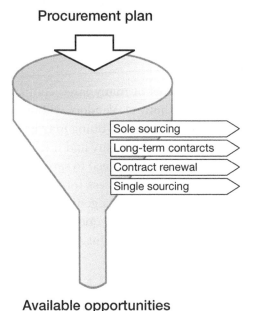

Procurement plan

Sole sourcing

Long-term contarcts

Contract renewal

Single sourcing

Available opportunities

idea of the scale of this type of limitation, in one mature oil production operation in a medium-income country known to the author, 36% of all routine capital expenditure committed for the forthcoming year was already allocated to support either contract extensions or contract renewals.

Fourth, significant portions of planned expenditure, particularly operational expenditure, may be **single sourced**, which may prevent new-entrant SMEs from participating in the opportunity. The practice of using one supply source without competitive bidding is justified on a variety of strategic grounds. This can include situations of urgency of a security, safety or environmental nature, or because international agreements have already established a single procurement source. Further to the oil production operation example cited above, commitments of operational expenditure in the same year to single and sole sourcing were 20%.

In summary, regardless of the capabilities and competitiveness of suppliers, in any forward procurement programme there will likely be parts of the anticipated expenditure already allocated and therefore not available to be put out to competitive tenders. To illustrate, for the same oil production operation cited above, of the total forward annual committed expenditure for 2010, 40% was already allocated, leaving 60% for competitive tender.

## e-procurement

The procurement procedures of many large companies can be difficult for local SMEs to penetrate. Vendors will usually first have to register with the company, and in so doing may have to pass certain standardised tests for financial viability and track record. To be considered for a tender, they may then need to satisfy a formal pre-qualification process. This may be a process formulated for a particular scope of work or purchase order, or a generalised voluntary process of pre-qualification with standardised questions, such as that used in parts of the oil and gas sector First Point Assessment Limited (FPAL) (see Box 6.2).

## Box 6.2 **FPAL vendor self-assessment pre-qualification**

Managed by the Achilles Group, First Point Assessment (FPAL) is the oil and gas industry's supply chain database in the UK, Netherlands and Ireland, with versions also being developed in Kazakhstan and Nigeria.

In this process, prospective vendors register by completing an online questionnaire. This describes the vendor's range of products and services, its capabilities and supply history. Supplier profiles are then made available online to around 80 purchasing members (oil and gas companies, and major contractors) who interrogate the list of suppliers in order to produce a short-list. FPAL operates in accordance with the EU Utilities Procurement Directives.

First Point Kazakhstan has been developed to register all suppliers to the oil and gas industry in Kazakhstan. Registered suppliers are visible to major purchasing companies and organisations in Kazakhstan. Further, through entry into the Achilles Global Directory vendors can market their products and services internationally.

The NipeX Joint Qualification System (NJQS) is designed to provide visibility and transparency in the contracts and procurement processes within the Nigerian oil and gas industry. The system is managed by Achilles in conjunction with the Nigerian National Petroleum Corporation and international oil and gas companies in Nigeria.

Clearly, if companies are going to limit themselves to selecting suppliers who have first registered themselves via this type of e-procurement process, regardless of the information required, these SMEs will need a sufficient Internet connection and evidence to satisfy requirements for information on, for example, health, safety and environment policies, quality assurance, tax clearance and audited accounts. By way of example, the mandatory information requirements for vendor registration for e-procurement are listed as follows:

1. Organisational chart (with names and responsibilities of staff)

2. Certificate of incorporation/registration

3. Schedule of directors, and statement of allotment of shares

4. Health, safety and environment (HSE) policies and procedures (where applicable)

5. Quality assurance/quality control (QA/QC) policies and procedures (where applicable)

6. Current tax clearance certificate

7. VAT registration certificate

8. A reference letter from the company's bank

9. Copy of agreements with original equipment manufacturers/ technical partners (where applicable)

10. Workmen compensation insurance and/or public (third-party) liability insurance (where applicable)

For small local companies (less so medium-sizes enterprises) a key constraint to satisfying these requirements is not so much the information itself, but the process of accessing the information; in particular, overcoming the bureaucratic obstacles to securing tax clearance and VAT certificates, reference letters, OEM agreements and liability insurance. Many smaller suppliers may not have attempted to register until they hear about the available opportunities (for example, via a local supplier forum or through website alerts). There is then a race to gather the right information to register, so that they are eligible to enter the subsequent selection process.

It is all the more important then that supplier fora and outreach programmes of SME support managed by oil, gas and mining companies or their lead contractors should include the early communication of these registration requirements, and provide assistance to enable local SMEs to navigate this first gate in the vender election process.

## Vendor pre-qualification

In a process of contractor selection, the subsequent ranking of prospective suppliers against pre-qualification questions can pose a further challenge to local SMEs. Common categories of questions used to pre-qualify vendors for minor service contracts or supplier agreements include:

- Technical capability and experience

- Health, safety and environment systems and performance

- Financial and corporate stability

- Human resourcing and capacity to do the work

Many pre-qualification questions are straightforward and most SMEs operating for a year or so would be quite capable of providing sufficient answers. However, for some questions, less experienced or smaller SMEs face challenges in achieving the mandatory or high enough scores to be selected through to a tender list.

Listed below are some typical evaluative criteria for assessing vendors that present just such challenges to local SMEs (in each case the vendor only scores the maximum of five if the cited criteria can be met):

- Vendor has annual **financial accounts** for the past three years and these confirm financial stability

- Vendor has more than five years' **experience** successfully managing a contact of this nature

- Vendor has experienced no change of ownership over the last five years

- Vendor has provided evidence that its **health, safety, security and environmental management systems** include techniques for risk assessment of all risks and effective implementing controls

- Vendor has produced evidence that key indicators of health and safety are all **improving**

- Vendor has won **awards** for its performance and work

Most pre-qualification processes exercise a minimum aggregate score, commonly 60%. Because of this, the more of these types of challenging question included in pre-qualification, or the more these questions are allocated higher relative weightings, the more challenging it is for local SMEs to be selected through to the tender list.

Further, it is not uncommon for the procuring company to introduce mandatory pass/fail thresholds for certain pre-qualification questions deemed risk or project critical. Two of the most common are as follows:

- The **vendor** has $x$ years' previous experience on a similar-natured contract

- The assigned **personnel** have a minimum of $x$ years' experience working on a similar nature contract

For a new-entrant or recent-entrant local SME, while the criteria for employing experienced personnel can be met if the company hires individuals with sufficient experience, the requirement for the company itself to have experience with a similar contract is more challenging, and can be prohibitive to the further progress of local SMEs in the selection process.

## Should pre-qualification criteria for local SMEs be relaxed?

These barriers to local SME participation in procurement raise the question of whether, in those developing countries or regions where there is an economic argument for increasing local content to create new jobs and protect local industries, pre-qualification criteria should be relaxed for local SMEs. One perspective, supported by the infant industry argument discussed in Chapter 1, suggests that this might not be entirely unacceptable, if certain procurement principles are maintained. The most important of these are:

- **Selectivity**. The parts of the pre-qualification evaluation criteria to be relaxed should be those that the vendor can readily overcome prior to submitting a formal tender, such as hiring specialist personnel or improving quality control systems

- **Contract execution to international standards**. In answering the more challenging pre-qualification questions on health, safety, environment and quality control, assurances are given by the vendor that contract execution will be delivered to the required technical and quality standards on contract award: for example, through additional management supervision, training or quality control by the client or by another, more experienced, domestic or foreign contractor

- **Contract award on a competitive basis**. Any relaxation at pre-qualification should not be carried through to the formal tender process, so that ultimately vendor selection is consistent with the principle of contract award on an internationally competitive basis

An alternative approach to relaxing the pre-qualification criteria would be for local SMEs to be allowed (or actively encouraged) to form strategic alliances with more experienced suppliers as a means to pass the mandatory questions, enhance their overall score and improve their overall chances of reaching the formal tender stage. Such alliances would then need to be carried through to the formal tender stage.

## Short-listing tenderers

The process for a local SME to pass successfully from a pre-qualification stage to formal tendering is not as simple as achieving a place in the first five or eight highest-scoring vendors. A range of criteria may be applied by the procurement entity to conclude a short-list of suppliers to invite to tender. These can include, *inter alia*:

- A high ranking in the formal pre-qualification process

- Vendors who have performed well in the previous provision of services or supply of goods

- Vendors who recently undertook other relevant pre-qualification or tendering processes, and scored well in these

- The results of outreach market surveys and analysis by procurement departments to identify suitable and capable local suppliers

- Information received from the execution of supplier development programmes that suggest certain SMEs are now fully capable

- The results of other parties' pre-qualification processes trusted by the procuring entity: for example, the FPAL vendor profiling cited in Box 6.2, or the master vendor lists of lead contractor firms

- The local knowledge of procurement professionals of which vendors are already capable (more common in remote locations or for services requiring equipment of limited local availability, such as earth-moving equipment)

Because of this complexity, and potential ambiguity, in determining tender lists, it is incumbent on procurement entities to be as transparent with prospective vendors as possible, and from the outset. Supplier fora and expositions, website communications and tender alerts should, wherever practicable, provide clarity on the forms of pre-qualification and other criteria for vendor selection to be applied.

## Communication

Spanning each of the above stages in the process of supplier selection is the quality of communication of the buyer with the local SMEs. It is a frequent complaint of local SMEs, particularly new entrants, that they did not know a tender was coming up, or that they had not realised that in order to pre-qualify they would need a minimum number of years of experience or established system of quality control. This lack of knowledge can have serious consequences for the owners of these enterprises, many of whom may have invested heavily in their ventures, only to find out later that their assumptions on the probability of winning work were far removed from reality. For the procuring entity, the ensuing resentment in the local area can undermine the reputation of the company and, in certain circumstances, take on a political dimension, affecting, for example, the approval of local authority operating permits.

A not uncommon practice that can fuel this type of risk is for the procuring company to announce publicly the dollar value of new capital investments. Such communications immediately raise expectations that local SMEs, and those who can get a business going quickly, have an opportunity to win part of this sum. The perception is invariably: 'how can we fail to win work with such large sums being invested in the local area?' Of course, the reality is very different.

The practice of publicising local content performance, and using metrics that can confuse the reader, is another cause of raised expectations in the local SME sector. Here the logic is: 'if local content is at 50% then why am I not getting any of it?' The answer may well be that the reporting metric being used is for suppliers tax-registered or located in the country, but that in reality a high proportion of this 50% is actually leaving the country to pay for imported goods and services.

In short, prudent procuring companies will be careful and transparent in communicating the available opportunities and provide clarity on the criteria and likelihood of vendors passing through each stage of the process of contract award. Box 6.3 summarises some of the ingredients of an effective procurement communications plan for local SMEs.

## Conclusions

This chapter has summarised some of the barriers to local SMEs accessing the procurement opportunities in the supply chains of oil, gas and mining companies. Suggestions have been made for improving communications and facilitating better access. Importantly, a rationale has been offered for retaining flexibility within procurement processes to be selective, focusing on sub-categories of expenditure that might support high-growth SMEs so that the jobs created are more sustainable and forward and backward linkages more likely.

## Box 6.3 Ingredients of a procurement communications plan for sourcing from local SMEs

1. **Supplier workshops**. 'Meet the buyer' workshop, fora and meetings held in the project area, with information on:
   a. The available expenditure sub-categories that offer opportunities for local SMEs, including:
      – Clarity on the level of confidence that these opportunities will be forthcoming, including whether budgets have yet been sanctioned (SME vendors are quite capable of understanding that the further into the future the expenditure the less clarity the buyer has over its procurement budget)
      – The anticipated probability of contract award, i.e. how much competition is anticipated
      – Clear explanation of why certain categories of expenditure is not being tendered, whether for reasons of single or sole sourcing, or because of outstanding long-term contractual arrangements
   b. Information on how to navigate the selection process
   c. Examples of successful local SMEs, and their key success factors
   d. Meet the buyers workshops may also include major contractors, so provide information on their subcontracting and supplier procurement processes
2. **Local office.** A local one-stop shop, where SMEs can visit to be informed of:
   a. Forthcoming procurement opportunities
   b. Requirements for entering and processing the selection process
   c. Where to go to receive training and advice
4. **Guidance.** Published SME information guides in local languages and via different media (dedicated website portal, print media, downloads, radio programmes) on how to navigate each stage of the selection process, including, if relevant:
   a. How to register as a vendor
   b. How to be e-procurement ready
   c. What industry standards will need to be met
   d. How to prepare bids and understand tender documents
5. **Contacts.** Useful contacts and information, for example:
   a. Peer SMEs who have been successful and are willing to share their experiences
   b. Details of SME financing and training institutions
   c. Toolkits on small business development: for example, the IFC SME Toolkit: www.ifc.org/ifcext/sme.nsf/Content/SME_Toolkit
6. **Feedback.** A commitment to provide feedback to all local SMEs on where they fell down in the selection process, with as much transparency as feasible on evaluation criteria

# 7

# SME development programmes

## Capacity building of SMEs to participate in procurement

Chapter 6 drew attention to what procuring entities can do to design procurement procedures and contractor selection processes and criteria to facilitate fair access to small- and medium-scale local enterprises to procurement opportunities. In this chapter, attention is turned to the other side of the equation: to the direct development of SME capacity to participate in procurement opportunities. The chapter has been prepared by **Robert Webster** of **CDC Development Solutions** (CDS)[1] in collaboration with the author. CDS specialises in SME capacity building and local supply chain development in the oil, gas and mining sector, with experience in Angola, Azerbaijan, UK, Guatemala, Russia, Kosovo, Equatorial Guinea and Jamaica.

---

1 CDC Development Solutions; www.cdcdevelopmentsolutions.org (accessed 16 June 2011).

# The SME perspective

The previous chapter demonstrated the importance of SMEs to a country's economy—especially the high-growth 'gazelles'—and highlighted the challenges local SMEs face in navigating the procurement procedures of the purchasing companies and competing with the market power of larger suppliers. In the context of procurement for oil and gas projects, Table 7.1 summarises the key challenges to local SME participation in procurement from a customer and a supplier perspective.

Table 7.1 **Challenges to local SME participation**

| Customer perspective | SME perspective |
| --- | --- |
| • Insufficient qualified local SME suppliers | • Producing reliable company and financial information |
| • Poor knowledge of qualified SMEs in local markets | • Access to potential procurement opportunities |
| • Higher cost of local suppliers | • Lack of technical competence |
| • Safety issues with local suppliers | • High unit cost of operations and lack of pricing acumen |
| • Local suppliers insufficiently responsive to needs and requests from customer | • Lack of health, safety and environment culture |
| | • Low level of planning and performance management capability |

In addressing these challenges, local SME development programmes have proved to be effective tools, in supporting local firms to strengthen their contract performance, and in being more aware of bidding opportunities, understanding how to be pre-qualified to access these opportunities and knowing what is needed to put together a successful bid.

Certain success factors are identifiable from past experience of SME development programmes. To varying degrees, such programmes need to:

- Provide access to markets through strategic targeting and planning

- Build effective business processes and technological capabilities

- Develop management capability and human capital

- Facilitate access to affordable finance

In the context of oil and gas developments, Figure 7.1 provides a simple model of the four focus areas of effective SME development programmes.

Figure 7.1 **Focus areas of an effective local SME development programme**

Source: adapted from model by CDC Development Solutions; www.cdcdevelopmentsolutions.org

**Access to markets**
- Market analysis
- Pre-qualification certification
- Formal and informal networking
- Facilitation of partnerships and alliances

**Access to finance**
- How-to guide for SMEs
- Training in preparing 'bankable' proposals
- Facilitation of access to finance: private banks, development finance institutions, private equity

**SME development programme**

**Management and human capital**
- Business planning
- Marketing and sales
- Management skills
- Human resources development and management

**Business processes and technology**
- Bids and contract performance
- Health, safety and environment processes
- Quality assurance
- Information technology

These success factors are discussed in turn below.

# Access to markets

The design of SME development programmes needs to include careful targeting in the choice of markets and choice of participating SMEs, and in aligning this supply side of the equation with the available procurement opportunities.

## Market targeting

Experience suggests that effective local SME support programmes target their assistance to SMEs with a realistic possibility of providing goods or services in their industry on a genuinely competitive basis. Thus, in less developed economies many such programmes focus on developing SMEs to supply standard, non-critical products and services, which are less complex, carry less risk to the customer and which require less technology, lower skill levels and less financial capital. In the extractive industries sector this might include the provision of manpower, catering services, transportation, security, light manufacturing, cleaning and so on.

With reference to the adapted Kraljic model discussed in Chapter 3, SME programmes targeted at these markets would lie somewhere between the 'Routine' quadrant and 'Leverage' quadrant (refer to Fig. 3.4 on page 70). To explain: although the services and products in question are 'routine' and low-risk in nature, it is the opportunity to leverage a long-term market for these services and products (in this case the operational procurement budget of local oil and gas operators or mining companies) that provides the opportunity for building SME capability. If the SME programme is successful, then subsequent procurement from these, now more capable, local suppliers would fall wholly in the 'Routine' quadrant, driving up the level of local content within overall procurement. In more developed economies, local SME support programmes might be targeted at any one of the quadrants in the adapted Kraljic matrix.

## Demand assessment

In deciding what markets and which SMEs to target for SME development, a further consideration is the availability of procurement opportunities of prospective customers. Chapter 6 highlighted the effect that sole sourcing, long-term contracts, contract renewal and single sourcing have on limiting the available opportunities. It is ineffective, for example, to target SME development programmes at markets in which, although the procuring company may have a long-term commitment to procure, it is the practice of the customer to always single source from a foreign or local supplier.

Effective SME development programmes are therefore invariably informed by some type of gap analysis of what goods and services are needed by the operators and what products either are or, more importantly, *could* be supplied by local SMEs. One route is to begin this analysis with an assessment of *demand*. Attention to the available opportunities in the short, medium and long term, and to what is already procured locally on a competitive basis, as well as a basic understanding of the local market, can generate a rapid, provisional list of goods and services that might form the basis for an SME development programme. Sources of information in compiling this demand-side assessment include:

- The forward procurement and contract plans of procuring entities, both the parent buyer and its lead contractors if they are procuring goods and services on behalf of the parent company

- Existing contracting strategies and local content plans of the procuring company

- Interviews with procurement managers and project managers

- Knowledge of product or service specifications, pre-qualification requirements and tender award criteria, e.g. HSE (health, safety and environment) requirements, quality control

## Supplier capabilities assessment

The *supply* side of the gap analysis begins with developing an understanding of the current local supplier market, including the number of firms involved, their current capabilities and potential to enhance these capabilities and their competitiveness over time, and the barriers and costs involved in doing so. As well as surveys of premises and interviews and questionnaires with managers and key workers, engagement with local chambers of commerce and business and trade associations can speed up the assessment process and help focus effort and resources on what would make for a practicable, high impact programme.

The type of data collected in such an assessment generally falls into three categories:

- **General business capabilities**. The types of information an investor might enquire about when considering investing in the growth potential of an established business, e.g. management quality, range of goods and services, current and future production capacity, HSE and quality control practices and past performance, financial status and access to finance, worker capabilities and capacity

- **Contract award requirements**. The specific product or service requirements that procuring entities will need local SMEs to satisfy to be eligible to tender for work, such as type, volumes and quality of product; and the requirements for entering and being successful in a competitive bidding process, including vendor registration, vendor pre-qualification and those areas of competition most relevant to winning a bid, e.g. price, management expertise, delivery

- **Key challenges to be overcome**. Those areas of assistance that will form the main thrust of the SME development programme: skills training, upgrading technologies, business processes and management systems, enabling access to finance, facilitation of business partnerships and alliances

Table 7.2 summarises the results of an illustrative demand/supply gap analysis to inform the design of a local SME development programme for the supply of different types of equipment to a mining operation in an emerging economy. In this illustration the programme is to be undertaken by a third-party specialist SME development organisation. In practice, such programmes can and

Table 7.2 **Results of gap analysis for local SME development programme: illustration of equipment supply to a mining operation**

Source: professional experience of Michael Warner, Local Content Solutions

| Equipment/material types | Local companies with potential capability | Current annual spend with local producers (US$ millions) | Potential annual spend following SME development programme (US$ millions) | Incremental value contributed (US$ millions) | Incremental value contributed (%) | Value for money (cost of SME programme per unit of incremental value contributed) | Key challenges to overcome |
|---|---|---|---|---|---|---|---|
| Caustic soda | 1 | 0.0 | 1.1 | 1.1 | 100.0% | **High** | Access to finance; pre-qual; quality control, health and safety, EMS |
| Ammonium sulphate | 1 | 0.0 | 0.2 | 0.2 | 100.0% | **High** | Pre-qual; quality control, health and safety, EMS |
| Ventilation ducting | 3 | 0.0 | 0.2 | 0.2 | 100.0% | Medium | Pre-qual; production volume; management competence |
| Grinding media | 2 | 10.2 | 22.5 | 12.3 | 54.7% | **High** | Competitive price; production volume; quality control |
| Explosives | 4 | 15.1 | 25.3 | 10.2 | 40.3% | **High** | Pre-qual; certification; quality control, health and safety |
| Mill liners | 1 | 0.3 | 5.8 | 5.5 | 94.8% | Medium | Access to raw materials; quality control |
| Lubricants | 3 | 3.3 | 4.5 | 1.2 | 26.7% | Medium | Price; quality control |
| PVC pipes | 2 | 2.2 | 3.9 | 1.7 | 43.6% | Low | Product range; production volume; management competence |
| Overalls and work clothes | 2 | 0.4 | 1.0 | 0.6 | 60.0% | Low | Quality control, health and safety |
| Steel products | 4 | 0.9 | 1.5 | 0.6 | 40.0% | Medium | Access to finance; pre-qual; quality control, health and safety, EMS |
| OTR tyre-retreading | 2 | 0.8 | 1.2 | 0.4 | 33.3% | Low | Throughput volume; quality control |
| Cement products/grout | 1 | 0.0 | 6.8 | 6.8 | 100.0% | Low | Pre-qual; quality control, health and safety, EMS |
| Quicklime and hydrated lime | 1 | 0.0 | 15.3 | 15.3 | 100.0% | Low | Pre-qual; quality control, health and safety, EMS |
| Wood products | 5 | 0.3 | 0.4 | 0.1 | 25.0% | Low | Price; quality control |

are implemented by an array of organisations, from specialist training and development companies and non-governmental organisations, to in-house SME development teams within the procuring
company (the parent company or its lead suppliers or contractors),
specialist agencies within the host government, or the same within
official development agencies.

In this illustration it is notable that the mining company may consider not only supporting clusters of local SMEs involved in producing a single product (e.g. explosives and lubricants), but also products
for which only one local SME has the potential to be a provider, such
as caustic soda and cement. This preferencing of a single SME for
support need not necessarily be considered anticompetitive. It all
depends on whether the SME, once developed, is exposed to foreign competition. What directing an SME programme or assistance
to a single local supplier does do, is raise the risk that an expectation is created within the recipient supplier and the procuring company that this SME will win work, so justifying the investment in
the programme. Table 7.2 clearly makes this assumption in the col-
umn anticipating the incremental value contributed. Of course, if
the intention is to grant a preference to local SMEs in the award of
these contracts—such as a 10% nominal price advantage—then the
procuring company will already have decided that some degree of
uncompetitive domestic preferencing is acceptable.

## Facilitation of partnerships and alliances

Partnerships, alliances and joint ventures are a particularly direct
way to improve the access of local SMEs to new opportunities. This
may involve backward and forward linkages with similar-sized local
or foreign SMEs, as well as forward linkages, through alliances,
with larger, more established, domestic and foreign suppliers and
contractors.

With reference to the extractive industries sector, as investments
within a country grow and these industries mature, national governments tend to shift from a focus on the *quantity* of local content to its
*quality*. Commonly this takes the form of policies and incentives for
import substitution directed towards those goods and services where
higher levels of value can be added in-country, for example through

manufacturing. Where the necessary technology and experience is lacking in-country, domestic SMEs may elect to develop preferred-supplier status with foreign suppliers, gain rights to product distribution or secure licences to repair and maintain foreign-manufactured equipment. Another option, and one sometimes favoured by national governments since it brings new technology in to the country, is to seek joint ventures with foreign or domestic OEMs (original equipment manufacturers) or with major service contractors (the TOFCO joint venture discussed in Chapter 4 provides an example).

With regard to joint ventures, it is most definitely not the case that the business development strategies of global OEMs and service contractors will always align with the ambitions of national governments to attract this type of inward investment. The proprietary nature of many of the specialist materials and equipment within the oil and gas development sector—chemicals, drilling and sub-surface equipment, production and processing technologies, etc.—precludes against joint ventures that have regulatory compliance rather than commercial viability as their core driver. However, where there is alignment—for example, in Brazil, where the size of the internal market is sufficiently large to warrant serious investments by international OEMs—a range of benefits can accrue to both domestic and foreign parties alike (see Table 7.3).

Table 7.3 **Possible benefits from domestic–foreign joint ventures**

| Joint venture benefits to foreign firms | Joint venture benefits to local firms |
|---|---|
| • Access to foreign markets, particularly if protected by local content requirements that include national ownership<br>• Potentially lower labour and logistics costs<br>• Access to knowledge of local legal and political environment<br>• Access to government opinion formers and decision-makers | • Access to foreign technology and expertise<br>• Access to financing due to financial stability of JV partner<br>• Access to foreign currency earnings<br>• Prestige and marketing advantage from association with an international firm<br>• Access to foreign markets via the JV partner |

Table 7.4 **Stages in the value chain for local SMEs to enter into strategic partnerships with international OEMs**

| Capability | Stage 1 | Stage 2 | Stage 3 | Stage 4 | Stage 5 | Stage 6 |
|---|---|---|---|---|---|---|
| | Sales | Operations | O&M | Assembly | Production | OEM |
| | Sales and technical advisers | Commercial operations (e.g. rental, storage, spares, installation) | Repair shop, maintenance service, local supply chain, training centre | Assembly and full O&M service | Production capability, local sourcing of components, testing | Full production and full testing facilities, engineering and design |
| Local content (approximate %) | 5–10 | 10–15 | 20–30 | 30–60 | 50–70 | 60–90 |

SME support programmes can be designed to be instrumental in facilitating connections between foreign and local firms, leading ultimately to joint ventures or other forms of alliance and strategic partnership. Programmes can include  investigations to identify potential partners, the hosting of formal or informal meetings to introduce organisations to each other, and awareness raising of newly developed SME capability with those trade bodies already engaged in matching international with domestic suppliers.

SME programmes can also provide advisory services to help local SMEs to understand where they are best placed to enter the value chain. Table 7.4 identifies six different stages in the value chain of an international OEM where local SMEs might participate in the supply of manufactured equipment, from sales to full-scale production and product testing. It is notable that the higher up the value chain, the higher the level of local content and the more value contributed to the national economy.

## Management and human capital

Management and human capital are challenges for SMEs worldwide, but particularly for the more developing economies in which the operations of oil, gas and mining companies increasingly take place. For example, many small business owners are excellent entrepreneurs—market visionaries and risk takers—but less good at budgeting, human resource planning and establishing management and quality control systems. Furthermore, finding capable middle managers to run emerging departments within a growing SME—marketing, human resources, etc.—is a common constraint. Managing relations with new senior managers and adequately rewarding their performance is a further challenge. This is so not least because the entrepreneurs in the original business (many without formal business training or tertiary education) are not always ready to relinquish the level of control or equity share necessary to attract and keep these new managers.

Accordingly, most effective local SME development programmes have at their core short training courses in business planning, strategic planning, marketing and sales, management skills and human resource management. Depending on market needs and preferences, such courses are typically one to three days. Some typical courses are given in Table 7.5.

Table 7.5 **Common business management training topics in SME development programmes**

| **Financial management** | **Planning** | **Marketing and sales** | **Human resource management** |
| --- | --- | --- | --- |
| • Cash management<br>• Internal controls<br>• Financing<br>• Budgeting | • Strategic planning<br>• Business planning<br>• Operational planning<br>• Risk management | • Market research<br>• Marketing strategy<br>• Branding<br>• Project development | • Recruitment<br>• Training<br>• Evaluation and incentives<br>• Benefits |

## Local vs. foreign trainers

Whether to use local or international trainers and advisers, and whether to outsource or in-house resources are important questions for the planners of SME development programmes to consider. For example, choosing local training organisations who have well-developed courses may be particularly effective, since these are likely to be more relevant to the realities of doing business in the country or region than material developed by overseas trainers. Further, building a training delivery market locally is a cost-effective way to ensure that consultancy and training services are available to SMEs on an affordable and ongoing basis, so assisting development of local SMEs over the long haul.

This said, specialist foreign trainers may be needed for products and services in which the local training and advisory market has no experience, or over which there is proprietary: for example, training in the maintenance or finishing of goods from OEMs.

## Outsourcing vs. in-house

Likewise, there are advantages and disadvantages to a procuring company electing to outsource an SME development programme rather than manage it in-house. Managing in-house potentially reduces the fixed costs of funding the programme (for example, if relying on existing human resources within the company). It also ensures close alignment with the company's pre-qualification requirements, specifications for required goods and service and procurement procedures, thus generating particular interest from local SMEs in the training.

In contrast, outsourcing such programmes may be beneficial where there is a need for training, advisory or pre-qualification services to be seen to be at arm's length from the procuring company: for example, to avoid charges of favouritism and unfair competition, or to reduce the risk of bribery within procurement decisions. Further, outsourcing SME development programmes is likely to result in a more comprehensive range of training and advisory services, compared with the limited services on offer from the procuring company itself based on the expertise of the current staff.

Perhaps most advantageous, outsourcing a programme arguably may generate longer-term commercial outcomes for local SMEs, since the provider is likely to have more freedom to offer training, advisory and certification services aligned with a broader market than just the one procuring company. This particular benefit is illustrated later in this chapter in Box 7.2, where an outsourced SME programme in Angola prepared SMEs to access procurement expenditure from across five oil and gas companies: BP, Chevron, ExxonMobil, Sonangol and Total.

## Charge vs. no charge

Whether or not an SME development programme uses trainers internal or external to the procuring company, or trainers who are local or foreign, programme planners will invariably face the question of whether or not to charge for the training and advisory services they offer. There are advantages and disadvantages to both options. This question is explored further in Box 7.1.

## Box 7.1 **To charge or not to charge—that is the question**

The design of a local SME support programme needs to balance two competing interests in deciding whether or not to charge its SME clients for its services. If such a programme has arisen because of the need to comply with mandated local content requirements (minimum targets, for example), or if the costs of such programmes are explicitly recoverable against production revenues or tax (as is not uncommon in many production-sharing agreements and other forms of concession agreements), or if such programmes are being funded directly through a government departmental agency budget, then there is an argument that these programmes should not be charged to the SMEs being assisted.

Countering this, however, are some sound economic reasons to consider charging for the training and advisory services provided, whether or not they are being mandated or subsidised. First, most SME development practitioners will argue that, when their clients are not asked to pay for training and advice, this can lead to several undesirable outcomes, including no-shows, the wrong participants or inattentive participants. Second, failure to charge may condition the recipient to under-value the service, thus undermining the very SME training and advisory market that will be needed to support the growth of these businesses in the long term. Third, in the shorter term, a SME programme that does not charge for services is likely to be directly undercutting the local training market and be legitimately accused of unfair competition.

Yet this is not necessarily an all-or-nothing decision. An SME programme can minimise its market distortion and still assist local businesses by using some combination of the following: (i) non-cash mechanisms, such as time-limited vouchers; (ii) subsidised training, with the level of subsidy made explicit so that future expectations are managed; (iii) involving local trainers and advisory firms whenever possible to build the local market; and (iv) introducing or communicating the incentives for participating in subsidised training and advisory services, most obviously the increased capability of the SME to win more work and expand.

In summary, the real question, then, is not whether to charge or not to charge, but how to deliver an effective SME development programme that fulfils its short- and long-term objectives without introducing market distortions.

# Business processes and technology

Building technology capability for SMEs is not only about information and communications technology. It is also about business processes and systems. Two of the most common needs of SME businesses are: (i) support to build the processes to navigate the procurement processes of customers; and (ii) assistance in developing health, safety and environment performance systems.

Local SMEs sometimes have little experience of how to pre-qualify or prepare a formal bid proposal, and can have quite lax policies and practices with regard to health, safety and environment management. Both of these challenges are serious impediments to winning business with international companies used to procuring from well-established suppliers operating to international industry standards. This said, experience has shown that local SMEs can be particularly responsive to assistance in these two areas, especially when motivated by a realisation that this can considerably improve the chances of capturing more work.

Unlike management training and to some extent training for HSE performance, training in how to pre-qualify and bid for contracts requires specialised, localised, training courses, developed specifically for the SME support programme. It is critical to enable local SMEs to achieve the necessary requirements to register with the procuring company and pre-qualify, thus becoming potentially eligible for consideration for formal bids. Note that becoming pre-qualified is no guarantee of making it on to a master tender list, and should never be sold as such (see Chapter 6 for a discussion on this point), but it is an essential step in the overall process of securing contracts, and one in which SME support programmes can have considerable impact in assisting SMEs to be 'bid ready'.

In cases where there is no formal requirements for pre-qualification, for example in periodic procurement of commodities such as bulk materials and routine products (standard chemical products, lubricants, fencing, etc.), one strategy is to build into the SME development programme a process of 'pre-qualification certification'. This involves the SME being audited against its capability to meet the requirements of the procuring company. Based on the results of this audit, support can then be given to the participating SME to bridge any gaps. Such an approach requires the procuring company to share with the parties providing the SME support what criteria they wish suppliers to meet and the scoring and weighting involved. An inventory of common pre-qualification criteria is given in Chapter 6 on pages 139-40. More generally, the requirements of an SME pre-qualification certification programme component might include the following:

- Proof of company incorporation

- Health, safety and environment policies and management system

- Quality assurance and quality control

- Tax clearance and product/service value-added tax registration

- Adequate insurance cover and financial security

- Proof of OEM and distribution rights

- Contract experience and reference

- Human resources and management policies and structure

- Level of local content within SME entity

Ultimately, the aim of this certification is to increase confidence in local SMEs on the part of the procuring companies, thereby improving their likelihood of being placed on tender lists. Equally important, the very process of an SME upgrading its capabilities to achieve this certification is likely to advantage it when engaged in formal bidding, rendering it more competitive against larger domestic and foreign firms.

Pre-qualification certification also provides an opportunity for local SMEs to access other similar markets. For example, CDC Development Solutions—the SME development organisation mentioned in the introduction to this chapter—helped construct a database of certified SMEs in Angola and Azerbaijan which is now used by BP and other oil and gas companies in these countries (see Box 7.2 for a case note from Angola). Sharing of the database has fostered improvements in cooperation in local procurement between oil and gas operators, while also reducing the burden and reputation risks on individual procurement departments.

### Box 7.2 **Case note on local SME pre-qualification certification in Angola**

Source: professional experience of Robert Webster, CDC Development Solutions; www.cdcdevelopmentsolutions.org

From 2005 through to 2010, CDC Development Solutions (a US non-profit organisation specialising in small business capacity-building programmes in the developing world) implemented an SME develop-ment programme in Angola, *CAE Apoio Empresarial*, on behalf of BP, Chevron, ExxonMobil, Sonangol and Total.

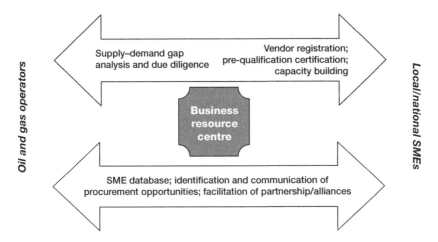

CAE operated from four offices across Angola, with headquarters in Luanda, the capital. The programme offered a suite of training courses (marketing, business planning, HSE performance, bids and contracts navigation, etc.) and provided supplementing advisory services to assist SMEs in becoming 'CAE certified'. CAE Pre-Qualification Cer-tification was based on criteria agreed with the oil and gas operating companies, providing them with an arm's-length, one-stop, pre-qual-ification system, as required. The programme also deployed a dedi-cated liaison staff to maintain an active supplier database of certified SMEs and link this to the procurement opportunities of the operators.

By 2010, the CAE programme had certified over 130 client SMEs and facilitated over US$200 million of local SME contracts. In January 2011, CDS transferred management and ownership of the programme to local staff and the Angola Chamber of Commerce, under the aus-pices of Sonangol, the national oil company.

Two other important technology areas for local SME assistance are **quality** and **information technology** management. Information technology cuts across a number of business functions: bid tracking, contract management, financial management, HSE performance, etc. While advanced IT technology, such as enterprise resource programmes or accounting packages can add significant value for more advanced firms, training on the more basic IT tools, such as use of Internet and desktop computer applications can also add considerable value to less advanced companies. Even simply helping some firms establish a web presence can be a 'quick win' for both the programme and the business.

# Access to finance for SMEs

Small and medium-sized enterprises the world over have challenges securing finance for working capital (to cover outgoings while awaiting payment for services rendered or goods supplied), bank loans (to invest in new plant, equipment and human resources) and risk capital (to support higher-trajectory business growth). The challenges are particularly acute for SMEs in developing economies, where local banks depend on relatively unsophisticated risk assessment criteria and tangible collateral, and where private equity options are few and far between.

This financing gap has come to be known as the 'missing middle' of private sector finance. On one side of this gap, micro-enterprises increasingly have access to credit through the proliferation of micro-credit schemes. On the other, larger national companies are well supported by local commercial banks or national or regional development banks. Thus ironically it is the real job-creators—the SME 'gazelles'—that remain under-served by appropriate financial products correctly adjusted for risk.

This challenge of access to affordable finance is highly relevant to SME development programmes. Although a supplier's credit rating and financial stability is a common requirement for pre-qualification to tender, and so relevant to SME support programmes designed to certify pre-qualification, without access to affordable finance the efforts of SME programmes to develop the capability of SMEs will have limited impact on the prospects for the business over the longer term. For these reasons, SME programmes frequently include a financing component, either directly, as part of the core programme, or as a facilitation service provided by the programme team.

Of course, there is only so much that an SME programme can do, and it may well be that regardless of the level of support for capacity building, the business remains 'unbankable' or the terms of the finance unacceptable. This said, there is much that SME programmes can do to improve access to finance. This includes, but is not limited to, the following:

- **Practical guidance on accessing finance**: (i) the financing options available and the role each plays, e.g. senior debt, junior debt, guarantees, equity; (ii) key procedural steps in applying for finance; (iii) the types of documentation typically required by banks and other financing institutions; (iv) the 'banker's' point of view, including how risk is assessed and terms adjusted accordingly; (v) key success factors in putting together a 'bankable' proposal; and (vi) current information on local bank financing offerings (rates, fees, etc.)

- **Training** in the preparation of bankable financing proposals and other aspects of SME financing

- **Bank networking**. Facilitating introductions for SMEs to local banks and other financing institutions. This can include types of 'speed dating' where SMEs summarise their company and financing needs to a range of banks on a one-on-one, quick-fire basis

- **Facilitating the development of customised financing models** and products tailored to the needs of their SME clients. Examples include:
  - **Debt financing**. Sector demand stimulates donors or governments to establish SME loan guarantee facilities or evidence generated from SME development programmes is used to more accurately assess loan risk, thus enabling local banks and public development finance institutions to lend on more favourable terms

- **Equity financing**. For example, a dedicated fund is established in support of an SME development programme (perhaps involving major companies or public development finance institutions, or both) which then takes medium-term (three to five years) equity positions in SMEs with high growth potential. The fund then deploys this influence on the board and through its voting rights to guide the growth of the business until it can exit its position at a profit and leave the business on a growth trajectory. The Anglo American 'Zimele' Supply Chain Fund is an example of this type of equity model. In 2009, this fund invested in five new companies bringing the total portfolio to 41, with US$8.9 million invested. These businesses employed 4,468 people and turned over US$68.4 million[2]

- **Subordinated equity fund**. A government financing agency or international development finance institution invests equity into a dedicated SME financing fund, with the intention of leveraging additional funds and enabling SME 'gazelles' to receive risk capital for business growth. For example, in the 1990s, the United States Agency for International Development (USAID) used a 'subordinated equity' model to attract other investors into SME risk capital funds for the risky, frontier markets of Eastern Europe. To establish such a fund, USAID would provide a grant to a fund manager to invest as seed capital in order to attract additional fund investors. The seed capital was 'subordinated' to these follow-on investors, who were assured a minimum investment return before the seed capital was repaid on the fund's liquidation[3]

---

2 Anglo American website; www.angloamerican.com/aal/development/social/socio-economic-development/enterprise-development, accessed 4 May 2011.

3 Professional experience of Robert Webster, CDC Development Solutions; www.cdcdevelopmentsolutions.org.

# Conclusions

This chapter has outlined what constitutes the core components of an effective SME development programme, whether such programmes are outsourced to specialist training, advisory and financing organisations, or managed in-house to the procuring company or contractors procuring on its behalf. The main components have been identified as access to markets, access to finance, capacity building for management and human capital, and support for business processes and technology. The importance of aligning local SME programmes with the available procurement opportunities and future markets, and assisting SMEs to ready themselves to navigate the many hurdles to contract award, have been emphasised.

It is worth noting that this topic is a considerable one, and that a single book can do no more than lay out some of the building blocks. Some suggested additional reading is as follows:

- 'A Guide to Getting Started in Local Procurement' by the International Finance Corporation[4]
- The SME and BEE Toolkits of the International Finance Corporation[5]
- UNDP's 'Growing Inclusive Markets' initiative[6]
- IFC 'Business Banking Knowledge Guide'[7]
- Shell Foundation 'Trading UP' initiative[8]
- Anglo American Zimele corporate enterprise development programme[9]

4 IFC, 'A Guide to Getting Started in Local Procurement'; commdev.org/content/document/detail/2741, accessed 16 August 2011.
5 IFC, 'Small and Medium Enterprise ToolKit'; www.ifc.org/ifcext/sme.nsf/Content/SME_Toolkit, accessed 16 June 2011.
6 UNDP, 'Creating Value for All: Strategies for Doing Business with the Poor', 2008; www.undp.org/gimlaunch, accessed 16 June 2011.
7 IFC, 'The SME Banking Knowledge Guide', 2009; www.ifc.org/ifcext/gfm.nsf/AttachmentsByTitle/SMEBankingGuidebook/$FILE/SMEBankingGuide2009.pdf, accessed 16 June 2011.
8 www.shellfoundation.org/pages/core_lines.php?p=corelines_content&page=trading, accessed 16 June 2011.
9 www.angloamerican.co.za/about-us/anglo-zimele.aspx, accessed 16 June 2011.

# 8

# Aid procurement

## An opportunity to stimulate private sector development through local supply chains

In 2009, total annual official aid stood at US$120 billion, with five countries contributing 62% of this: United States (US$28.7 billion), France (US$12.4 billion), Germany (US$12.1 billion), United Kingdom (US$11.5 billion) and Japan (US$9.5 billion).[1] Although these five are dominant in the overall patterns of official aid, as a proportion of a country's gross national income (GNI), the smaller donors, in particular Denmark, Norway and Sweden, contributed relatively higher volumes. Most generous was Sweden at 1.12% of GNI, a figure materially higher than the long-held United Nations target of countries contributing 0.7% of GNI.

The majority of this aid is discharged through bilateral agreements with governments in the developing world. But significant portions are also channelled, not through bilateral aid programmes, but

---

1 Budget4Change country profiles (interactive statistics); www.budget4change.org/countryprofile/united-kingdom, accessed 18 April 2011.

through multilateral institutions such as the World Bank Group and United Nations agencies. Influence over how aid is spent in these multilateral institutions is tied to voting rights, in part proportioned to the volumes of aid contributed.[2]

With the substantial volumes of bilateral and multilateral public expenditure on aid come responsibilities. To be as impactful as possible in effecting poverty reduction, peace-building or economic development, aid agencies and departments seek to apply transparent procurement practices that are results-focused and carry incentives to deliver projects and programmes on time and on budget. Such performance-driven aid, for example, is already operationalised within the UK Department for International Development through its declared commercial approach to procurement,[3] as it is in a number of other bilateral and multilateral development agencies, including USAID and the International Bank for Reconstruction and Development (IBRD).

But this recognition of the need for a commercially driven approach to procurement for aid programmes suggests ongoing reconnaissance of the commercial practices in other industries where procurement and outsourcing form a large component of total company expenditure. Drawing on the procurement experiences described in this book in the oil, gas, mining and infrastructure sectors, the question needs to be asked: could procurement departments do more to position aid expenditure so that it not only delivers primary development outcomes, but concurrently stimulates secondary outcomes in the form of sustainable jobs and competitive local firms aligned with the mission of these agencies to support private sector development?

2 At time of writing, voting power at the IBRD (World Bank) was: United States (15.9%), Japan (6.8%), Germany (4.0%), China (4.4%), France (3.8%) and the United Kingdom 3.8% (Wikipedia, 'World Bank Group'; en.wikipedia.org/wiki/World_Bank_Group, accessed 18 April 2011).

3 DFID, *Procurement Can Make It Happen: A DFID Commercial Strategy* (Final Version; London: Department for International Development, 2008; www.dfid.gov.uk/Documents/procurement/dfid-comm-strategy-proc.pdf).

# Quality in aid procurement

A common mantra of those who manage aid budgets is that it is not simply the volume of aid that determines the extent to which development goals are met, but also its quality. It is well understood that the design of aid procurement processes and contract terms are critical factors in delivering quality aid—aid that not only delivers medical equipment, education, training or infrastructure on time, to budget and with the intended impact, but that also, in the very act of purchasing goods and services, stimulates new jobs in the local economy. This logic applies equally to aid projects procured directly by donor governments, as it does to projects funded by these donors but procured indirectly by multilateral agencies, public procurement departments of partner governments, or companies in receipt of development finance.

Yet currently there is perhaps a rather narrow view of what these procurement procedures and common clauses can achieve by way of stimulating private sector development—a view that mirrors the way in which host government regulators of local content are preoccupied with setting local content targets and granting price advantages to domestic suppliers. Specifically, are development agencies omitting to utilise bidding processes to provide incentives for primary contractors to not only hire local staff and purchase goods of domestic origin, but also proactively develop the capability, capacity and competitiveness of these local suppliers as an explicit objective of contract execution?

To illustrate where thinking on the role of aid procurement processes in stimulating private sector development currently lies, the following section outlines the standard approach of the World Bank to domestic preferencing in the procurement of goods.

# World Bank approach to local preferencing in procurement

The 2010 version of the Standard Bidding Documents of the World Bank for the procurement of goods and related services lays out in detail model tender documents and pro forma conditions of contract.[4] The documents are applicable to competitive bidding in projects financed in whole or in part by loans for credits from the International Bank for Reconstruction and Development (IBRD) and International Development Association (IDA).

One of the stated underlying principles for procurement in World Bank projects is 'the Bank's interest in encouraging the development of domestic contracting and manufacturing industries in the Borrowing country'.[5] To this end, although the aforementioned 2010 Standard Bidding Document contains the stated presumption that preference for goods manufactured in the purchaser's country[6] will not be a factor in bid evaluation, provisions are also made for exemptions from this presumption. Eligibility for domestic preference includes procurement of domestically manufactured goods and of locally manufactured equipment within larger contracts (other than turnkey contracts). Eligibility for domestic preferencing is for member countries that both fall below a specified threshold of gross national product per capita (US$995 in 2010)[7] and where the

---

4 World Bank, 'Procurement of Goods, Standard Bidding Documents', Washington, DC, May 2010; web.worldbank.org/WBSITE/EXTERNAL/PROJECTS/PROCUREMENT/0,,contentMDK:21351162~menuPK:84284~pagePK:84269~piPK:60001558~theSitePK:84266~isCURL:Y,00.html, accessed 16 June 2011.
5 World Bank, 'Guidelines, Procurement of Goods, Works and Non-Consulting Services', Para 1.2 (p. 2), January 2011; web.worldbank.org/WBSITE/EXTERNAL/PROJECTS/PROCUREMENT/0,,contentMDK:20060840~pagePK:84269~piPK:60001558~theSitePK:84266,00.html, accessed 23 June 2011.
6 Meaning the country of the entity purchasing the goods and related services, which is usually the recipient country.
7 Personal communication with A. Motamedi, Senior Procurement Specialist, Procurement Policy and Services Group, Operations Policy and Country Services, World Bank, 25 April 2011.

borrower has requested such an arrangement and is included in the procurement plan for the project.

Where this exemption is exercised, calculation of the margin of preference on contract award to domestically manufactured goods uses a form of the 'most economically advantageous tender' method discussed in Chapter 5. Importantly, and consistent with the principles underpinning use of a correction factor, the price preference for local suppliers is applied only for the expressed purpose of making contract award. For the procurement of goods, the evaluation criteria are as follows.

Bids are first classified into one of three groups:

- **Group A**. Bids where the ex-works/factory (EXW) price is >30% for goods manufactured in the purchaser's country (labour, raw materials and components) and the production facility has been engaged in manufacturing or assembling such goods at least since the date of bid submission

- **Group B**. All other bids offering goods manufactured in the purchaser's country

- **Group C**. Bids offering goods manufactured outside the purchaser's country that have been imported or will be imported

Once classified, bids are compared to identify the lowest, technically acceptable bid price in each of the three groups.[8] If a bid from Group A or Group B is the lowest, then this bid is selected for award. However, if the lowest bid is from Group C (i.e. the bid contains no local content), then:

---

8  The price quoted for goods in bids of Groups A and B include duties and taxes paid or payable on the basic materials or components purchased in the domestic market or imported, but exclude the sales and similar taxes on the finished product. The price quoted for goods in bids of Group C is the CIP price, which is exclusive of customs duties and other import taxes already paid or to be paid (World Bank, 'Guidelines, Procurement of Goods, Works and Non-Consulting Services', Appendix 2, p. 43).

- The prices of all Group C bids are elevated by 15% of the CIP price (carriage and insurance paid),[9] and then

- The price-adjusted bids in Group C are compared with the lowest-priced bid in Group A, and the resulting lowest-priced bid awarded the contract.

The definitions used are important, and are as follows:

- 'Goods manufactured in the purchaser's country' is defined in the Price Schedule template as that percentage of ex-works/factory price that is 'cost of local labor, raw materials and component from with [*sic*] origin in the Purchaser's Country'

- The term 'origin' is defined in the Instructions to Bidders as meaning 'the country where the goods have been mined, grown, cultivated, produced, manufactured or processed; or, through manufacture, processing, or assembly, another commercially recognised article results that differs substantially in its basic characteristics from its components'

- 'Goods' is defined in the same Instructions as meaning 'commodities, raw materials, machinery, equipment, and industrial plants; and "related services" . . . such as insurance, installation, training and initial maintenance'

Box 8.1 provides a simplified illustration of the method.

For evaluating bids for service contracts the methodology differs slightly, with a margin of 7.5% to domestic contractors, subject to their provision of additional information on eligibility including national ownership.

The World Bank's approach to domestic preferencing is notable for at least three reasons. First is the choice of eligibility criteria applied to determine whether domestic preferencing is to be allowed. It is questionable, perhaps, whether a GNP per capita threshold is the most effective criterion to apply (notwithstanding the criterion of

9 CIP: seller pays for carriage and insurance to the named destination point, but the risk passes when the goods are handed over to the first carrier.

Box 8.1 **World Bank method for preferencing local suppliers in procurement: a simplified illustration**

---

Based on World Bank Standard Bidding Documents for Procurement of Goods (2010),[a] where:

>Group A, Bid #1 = US$2.0 million
>Group A, Bid #2 = US$2.3 million
>
>Group C, Bid #3 = US$1.9 million
>Group C, Bid #4 = US$1.8 million

- Lowest Group A bid is Bid #1 (US$2.0 million)
- 15% CIP adjustment to Group C bids results in Bid #3 at US$2.2 million and Bid #4 at US$2.1 million
- Contract award to Bid #1 (US$2.0 million)

a   World Bank, 'Procurement of Goods, Standard Bidding Documents'.

---

'ownership' for service contractors). Although the intention is clear, such a broad criterion might possibly preclude a member country whose GNP per capita is higher than this threshold from proposing a viable 'infant industry' argument (defined in Chapter 1) as justification to protect a particular domestic industry.

Second, the formula for preferencing domestic manufacturers offers two layers of granularity with respect to the extent to which the level of local content might play a part in bid evaluation. With regard to goods, the formula grants contract award either to: (i) a bidder who can combine the lowest price with 'some' local content (Group B); or (ii) a bidder who has greater than 30% local content and, when a 15% price elevation is assigned to bids that have no local content, is nominally the lowest price (Group C). More refinement in the evaluation criteria might provide greater incentives for bidders to innovate to maximise local content.

Third, the preference for domestic manufacturers of goods is focused on the monetary proportion of local content within a bid. The method appears to give little weight to how contract execution might impact the broader concept of local content 'development': that is, the quality of a bid in terms of its positive effect on local skills or domestic supplier capability and competitiveness or its potential to generate a significant or targeted economic multiplier effect within the economy.

# Aid expenditure as a private sector stimulus

With reference to the third observation above, recent experience by a number of multinational oil, gas and mining companies operating in developing countries, validated by a growing number of independent economic studies, demonstrates that expenditure on goods and services can provide a stimulus to the local private sector, not just in increasing temporary employment or filling local order books in the short term (i.e. in increasing local content), but also in developing and growing the long-term competitiveness of domestic suppliers. For a detailed example of this type of local content 'development', please refer to Chapter 4 on the Poinsettia Case Study in Trinidad and Tobago. These additional, long-term economic effects take two forms, as follows.

First, although significant volumes of procurement expenditure on goods and services often go to foreign contractors and suppliers, the portion that remains in the host economy invariably generates an economic multiplier effect of between one and three times the original expenditure (sometimes more if the country is particularly poor with a large informal sector).

Second, if well managed and directed, this same procurement expenditure can strengthen the competitiveness of local suppliers, driving their adoption of new skills and technology and improving health, safety and environmental performance. This in turn can lead to their expansion into new markets, the creation of forward and backward linkages and ultimately the creation of long-lasting jobs.

The commercial experience of the extractive industries also demonstrates that the choice of procurement process and tender evaluation criteria are determinants of the magnitude and quality of these effects on private sector development. In this sector, for example, as described in Chapters 3, 4 and 5, ever more stringent host-country local content requirements, commercial cost and schedule pressures, and the need to protect corporate reputations, are combining to encourage oil and mining companies to rethink the way they procure goods and services. New contracting strategies and procurement tactics are being formulated explicitly to manage the commercial risks presented by lower-quality local contractors, and this is being done in part by incentivising major contractors to build the capabilities, performance and competitiveness of local suppliers. In essence then, it is the commercial risks arising from the pressure to increase local content that is driving innovation to develop the capabilities and competitiveness of domestic supply chains through contract tendering and execution.

## Current procurement practices

The discipline of contracting and procurement is complex. It brings together project managers, contract engineers, procurement officers, contract and competition lawyers, and, increasingly, social and environmental performance advisers. The procurement profession within official aid expenditure, like the procurement profession as a whole, is heavily dependent on model and recycled documents: for example, the suite of model FIDIC pre-qualification documents, invitations to tender and conditions of contracts; the standard bidding documents of the World Bank (see above) and Asian Development Bank,[10] and the model general bid documents and conditions of contract used by bilateral development agencies.

With regard to these bid documents, as seen with the illustration from the World Bank above, model instructions for tenderers and tender evaluation criteria do not appear to request or reward proposals from bidders that detail how contract execution might lead to local supply chains becoming more capable and competitive, or that target their economic multiplier effect. What these standard documents do sometimes request are:

10 Refer, for example, to the 2010 model conditions of contract for building and engineering works, harmonised between FIDIC and the multilateral development banks; www1.fidic.org/resources/contracts/mdb, accessed 16 June 2011.

- Tender lists that exclude foreign bidders

- Targets for a fixed proportion of contract value to be subcontracted to locally registered companies

- Nominal price advantage for locally registered or nationally owned suppliers (see Box 8.1)

- Procurement guidelines promoting labour-intensive and appropriate technologies or community participation[11]

While these procurement practices may increase job opportunities in the short term, they also carry a number of risks, from elevating project costs and endangering project schedules and quality, to locking in unproductive practices and undermining local private sector competitiveness (refer to Chapter 1 on local content and protectionism).

## New procurement tactics

Human resource quality and efficiency is a priority in many, if not all, official development assistance agencies (politicians believing that the public wish to see their taxes go towards aid projects and not staff salaries). Given these political constraints, it is unclear whether there are sufficient procurement professionals within the main agencies experienced in modifying model procurement documents and contract terms so that, within the applicable competition and anti-discrimination rules, expenditure on aid projects can be positioned to stimulate private sector development in local supply chains. The challenge is not only the need to modify the standard instructions to tenderers and evaluative criteria, it is also knowing how to do this in ways that align with a country's poverty reduction strategy, economic development plan and other plans and strategies that govern

11  For example: World Bank, 'Guidelines Procurement Under IBRD Loans and IDA Credits', Washington, DC, May 2010; siteresources.worldbank. org/INTPROCUREMENT/Resources/ProcGuid-10-06-RevMay10-ev2. pdf, accessed 16 June 2011.

the priorities for how aid is to be directed to support private sector and industrial development.

And yet, as seen in other chapters in this book, there are a wide range of procurement principles, strategies and tactics that could be brought to bear on this challenge, if only the resources and skills were in place. These include:

- **Procurement strategies** for higher-value contracts that bundle procurement opportunities to incentivise learning and technology transfer from large international or domestic contractors to lower-tier domestic suppliers, or that unbundle contracts to broaden the opportunities for smaller-scale local suppliers

- **Pre-qualification criteria** that impart the message that training, fair access for local suppliers, local supplier development, economic multipliers and dual purpose infrastructure will be considerations in contract award

- **Tender instructions** and requests for proposals/quotes that require bidders to submit innovative proposals on the training of nationals, fair local sourcing, supplier development, maximum economic multipliers, dual-purpose infrastructure and business incubation

- Sufficient weight given to local content and private sector development proposals in **tender evaluation criteria**, including use of pass/fail gates

- Use of optional innovation budgets or post-award **provisional sums** to ensure that bidders' proposals on supplier development do not undermine the bid price competitiveness

- **Contract payment terms** and reporting metrics that reward or measure, not only the level of local content achieved (as in the World Bank standard bidding documents), but also improvements in local supplier competitiveness and marketability, e.g. HSSE performance, new contracts won

# Private sector development outcomes

Application of these types of procurement strategy and tactics, especially in relation to higher-value procurement contracts involving lower domestic supply chains, can play an important part in delivering the goals of international donors and host governments for private sector development, in particular:

- Skills training that increases **the long-term earning potential** of employees, subcontractors and temporary workers

- Local suppliers achieving certification to international quality standards and thus better able compete locally or **access global markets** (ISO 14000, ISO 9001, occupational health [e.g. OHSAS], welding [e.g. ASME codes], project management certifications, etc.) (refer also to Chapter 7)

- Productivity and capability improvements that enable local suppliers to **compete in regional or international markets**, e.g. moving up the value chain from repair and maintenance to finishing or manufacturing

- Community-based micro and small businesses incubated within larger, long-term service or management contracts, and then launched as **free-standing local enterprises**

- Alliances between local suppliers and large international or domestic suppliers to secure **technology transfer** and access global supply chains, e.g. local manufacture and regional exports, or local consultants marketing themselves internationally through UK-based consultancy firms

- Project-related **infrastructure that has a 'dual purpose'**, e.g. the transformation of temporary access roads during civil construction work into permanent rural feeder roads

## Conclusions

This chapter has raised the question of how much further the procurement processes of official development agencies might go in stimulating private sector development through the expenditure of billions of dollars of aid on the purchase of goods and services. In summary, realising enhanced private sector development through aid procurement requires at least three steps, as follows:

1. Where competition rules allow, for higher-value contracts, formulate model pre-qualification questions, invitations to tender and bid evaluation criteria to optimise local content with consideration to the trade-offs, and solicit cost-effective proposals from lead suppliers to maximise the economic multiplier impact of their activities to leave a legacy of enhanced local skills and strengthened subcontractor/supplier capability and competitiveness

2. Augment standardised bidding documents to fit local circumstances through a clear understanding of the capabilities and growth potential of local supply chains and the priorities for private sector development of the donor agency and its partner governments

3. Build a cadre of procurement professionals within development agencies and their partners with skills to formulate procurement strategy and adapt model documents, and able to play an associated role in bid evaluations, contract negotiations and contract performance management

# 9

# Metrics and measurement

## Unpacking the performance reporting of local content and local supplier development

Whether for reasons of compliance or reputation, oil, gas and mining companies and government regulators increasingly communicate their performance in local content, and like to demonstrate how the figures and trends are ever upwards. But just how much credibility should be placed in these figures, and on these trends?

This final chapter investigates different metrics for defining and reporting on local content, and contrasts each for their accuracy, comprehensiveness and ease of administration. But let us begin by laying to rest a few myths about local content reporting.

# Myths of local content reporting

The most obvious myth associated with reporting local content is the presumption that the higher the level of local content recorded the better. The question here is 'better for whom'? In practice, higher levels of local content may well have an impact on the interests of other stakeholders. For example, higher levels of local content can, depending on circumstances, lead to:

- The erosion of commercial value for investors and developers and/or greater risks to project delivery and operational performance

- A fall in levels of inward investment and technology transfer by international suppliers and contractors

- A decline in the international competitiveness of domestic industry

- Loss or delay in the accumulation of national (state) revenues

- Unsustainable dependence of a local economy on the oil, gas or mining company for jobs and order books

These trade-offs are discussed and modelled in Chapters 1 and 2. In contrast, this chapter focuses solely on the impact of local content *reporting* per se. There are two particular myths associated with the reporting of local content statistics, which deserve attention.

The first is that reporting higher levels of local content necessarily means that performance is improving. In practice, a high level of reported local content, whether at the local community level or regionally or nationally, can simply be a reflection of the type of metric being deployed.

To illustrate, it seems likely that, in Kazakhstan, application of the current formula for reporting local content in the purchase of goods of domestic origin[1] (which requires a certificate proving such origin)

---

1   Republic of Kazakhstan, General Provisions: Single Methodology to Calculate Kazakhstani Content Pertaining to Purchased Goods, Works and Services, September 2009.

will lead to a fall in the reported levels. Until the formula was introduced, subsoil development companies were reporting local content using their own formulae. Invariably, these metrics did not require a certificate proving the origin of goods or services.

Further, some company metrics were based on 'committed' expenditure, not 'actual' expenditure as required under the new formula: that is, on the planned value of goods and services, not the actual value of goods ordered or services delivered.

Lastly, the regulatory effort involved in certifying goods and producers is a significant bureaucracy hurdle, and may well result in a period of under-reporting while the system of certification matures. (This last error can of course be removed if the local content data reported are derived exclusively from that subset of expenditure for which such certificates exist.)

Taking these considerations together, a developer who reported 45% aggregate local content in 2008 for the purchase of goods, and two years later under the new reporting regulations reported 23%, may have actually achieved a higher level of local content in 2010, not lower.

In summary, when metrics are undergoing revisions, simply reporting the headline figures for local content, without explaining the context, carries a significant potential for error.

But what of 'trends'? Surely, even if revising a metric introduces ambiguities over time, an increasing or decreasing trend in local content using the 'same' metric should be reliable. Again, however, this is not necessarily so, and leads us to the second myth: that an averaged linear trend in local content is a reliable indicator of performance.

The problem is that the development and operation of oil, gas and mining concessions are characterised by periods of elevated capital expenditure. Thus an apparent upwards linear trend over time may actually reflect no more than the different levels of local content able to be achieved in capital versus operational expenditure.

Figure 9.1 shows a typical flow of capital and operational expenditure across a 24-year concession. Plotted against these flows is the headline local content figure for all expenditure on bought-in goods and services (capital and operational expenditure combined). In this scenario there is no assumed increase in the capability or competitiveness of domestic suppliers over time. In other words, the real rate of improvement in performance is zero.

Figure 9.1 **Inherent variability in local content**

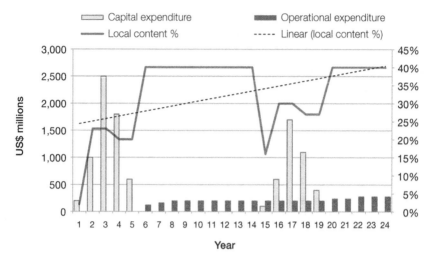

The apparent upwards average linear trend seen in Figure 9.1 is a consequence of both proportionately less expenditure going to domestic suppliers during periods of capital investment, and this capital spend being committed early in the lifespan of the concession. As is common in these industries, especially in emerging economies with undeveloped manufacturing capacities, during periods when capital projects are being executed, a higher overall share of annual expenditure will go on equipment and materials purchased from specialist foreign suppliers, such as rotating equipment, 'long-lead' items that require the manufacture of parts to specification, and exotic materials and drilling and excavation equipment where the supplier market is limited.

Figure 9.2 presents a modified scenario. It shows what happens if local content performance improves by 5% year on year as a result of vendor development programmes delivered by the developer, lead contractors and state agencies. Note that the 'real' trend in local content performance here is the variance between the two averaged trends, and that in Figure 9.1 the 'real' trend is actually flat.

Figure 9.2 **'Real' vs. 'inherent' trends in local content**

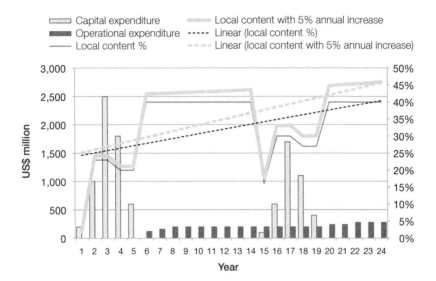

A final observation on trends is to understand how 'scale' can affect results. From years 5 to 6 in Figure 9.1 we see a significant jump in local content from 21% to 42%; and in contrast, in years 14 and 15, a dramatic fall from 44% to 18%.

These trends, apparent only when looked at from a medium-term perspective, have little to do with how successful the company, local industry or state agencies might be in building industrial capability and competitiveness. The initial rise in years 5 to 6 is simply a consequence of shifting from a project delivery to operational mode, with a relatively higher proportion of expenditure subsequently going on local site-based services and orders for locally produced materials.

Likewise, the sharp fall across years 14 to 15 results from the onset of a new period of capital investment, with early expenditure by the developer on expensive 'long-lead' equipment and exotic materials, procured directly from foreign manufacturers.

With regard to both of these myths, what can be concluded is that reporting local content is more than simply the reporting of the figures themselves. It is about understanding, and above all explaining, precisely what it is that the metric is measuring, and what is happening in the wider economic or business environment that might be influencing the figures and trends.

# A typology of local content metrics

Tables 9.1 and 9.2 present a typology of local content metrics. These metrics are currently used, or being considered, by regulators and companies in the oil, gas and mining sectors. The inventory is non-exhaustive, but includes some of the more common metrics, as well as those with potential to influence other regulators around the world in the future, such as the certification-based metrics being adopted in Brazil and Kazakhstan at the time of writing.

Table 9.1 lists metrics that measure local content. Table 9.2 lists metrics to measure the development of local suppliers through on-the-job training, management supervisions, quality control, investment, education and so on.

Each table classifies the metrics under three headings:

- **In-house**. The workforce on the payroll of the development or operating company

- **Services and goods**. Metrics that can be applied to either the provision of services or supply of goods

- **Specific metrics**. Apply only to one or the other of goods or services

The inventory of supplier development metrics in Table 9.2 is further classified into **input** metrics, such as training hours and capital investment, and **output** metrics, such as improvements in labour productivity and price competitiveness.

The inventory of output metrics in Table 9.2 covers only a narrow set, but this includes some important examples along with two new metrics that the author considers are being overlooked and yet should form a central part of any company's or authority's long-term reporting on local content (see later in this chapter). For a more comprehensive list of output metrics, the reader is referred to a forthcoming report by the World Business Council for Sustainable Development prepared by the Dalberg consultancy firm.[2]

page 196 ➔

2 See World Business Council for Sustainable Development, *A Framework for Dialogue on National Market Participation and Competitiveness* (Geneva: WBCSD, forthcoming late 2011).

Table 9.1 **Typology of local content metrics**

| Metric | Key feature | Information source | Supply chain penetration | Stage of procurement | Expenditure category | Confidence in data | Simplicity to administer | Economic accuracy* |
|---|---|---|---|---|---|---|---|---|
| **In-house** | | | | | | | | |
| # FTE national citizens employed as % of total | Head count | Human resources data | n/a | n/a | OPEX | Good | Simple | Erroneous |
| # FTE national citizens in senior, supervisory and skilled positions (or other job or grade disaggregation) | Head count by job type | Human resources data | n/a | n/a | OPEX | Moderate | Simple | Proxy |
| # man-hours of national labour per year | Man-hours | | n/a | n/a | OPEX | Good | Simple | Proxy |
| $ value of wages, benefits and social taxes paid to FTE national citizens employed as % of total | Wages | Human resources data | n/a | n/a | OPEX | Good | Moderate | Erroneous |
| $ value of wages, benefits and taxes paid to FTE national citizens in senior, supervisory and skilled positions (or other job or grade disaggregation), as % of sub-total | Wages by job type | Human resources data | n/a | n/a | OPEX | Moderate | Moderate | Accurate |
| $ value of wages, benefits and social taxes paid to FTE national citizens employed and $ value of social taxes and expenses paid to expats, as % of total | National wages and expat expenses/taxes | Human resources data | n/a | n/a | OPEX | Good | Moderate | Accurate |

* *Economic accuracy*—meaning the accuracy of data in measuring or reporting the actual financial contribution to the economy. For example, it would be 'erroneous' to report that an 80% headcount for nationals in a contract implies that most of the wage costs for the contract stayed in the economy. If the contract involved expats, it is possibly that 80% national headcount might equate to only 20% of the total wage costs.

| Metric | Key feature | Information source | Supply chain penetration | Stage of procurement | Expenditure category | Confidence in data | Simplicity to administer | Economic accuracy* |
|---|---|---|---|---|---|---|---|---|
| **Services and goods** | | | | | | | | |
| # nationally registered vendors on company vendor register | Vendor register | Company vendor register | 1st tier | Vendor registration | CAPEX or OPEX | Good | Simple | Erroneous |
| # community-based vendors on company vendor register | Vendor register—community | | 1st tier | Vendor registration | CAPEX or OPEX | Moderate | Moderate | Erroneous |
| # contracts awarded to nationally registered vendors | Tax registered | Contracts Plan | 1st tier | Commitments (contract award) | CAPEX or OPEX | Good | Simple | Erroneous |
| # contracts awarded to nationally owned vendor (>50% equity), as % of total | National equity | Contracts Plan/ National Company Register | 1st tier | Contract award | CAPEX or OPEX | Poor | Complex | Erroneous |
| $ value of contracts awarded to vendors with office address (PO or invoice) within the country, as % of total | Office address—national | Contracts Plan/ Company Vendor Register | 1st tier | Commitments (award) or actuals (invoice) | CAPEX or OPEX | Good | Simple | Erroneous |
| $ value of contracts awarded to vendors with office address (PO or invoice) within local/affected community or region, as % of total | Office address—regional/community | Contracts Plan/ Company Vendor Register | 1st tier | Commitments (award) or actuals (invoice) | CAPEX or OPEX | Good | Simple | Erroneous |
| $ value of contracts awarded to nationally registered vendors | Tax registered | Contracts Plan/ Company Vendor Register | 1st tier | Commitments (award) or actuals (invoice) | CAPEX or OPEX | Good | Simple | Proxy |
| $ value of contracts awarded to community-based vendors | Community-based | Contracts Plan/ Company Vendor Register | 1st tier | Commitments (award) or actuals (invoice) | CAPEX or OPEX | Moderate | Simple | Erroneous |
| $ value of contracts awarded to nationally owned vendor (>50% equity), as % of total | National equity | Contracts Plan/ National Company Register | 1st tier | Commitments (award) or actuals (invoice) | CAPEX or OPEX | Poor | Complex | Erroneous |

| Metric | Key feature | Information source | Supply chain penetration | Stage of procurement | Expenditure category | Confidence in data | Simplicity to administer | Economic accuracy* |
|---|---|---|---|---|---|---|---|---|
| **Services-specific** | | | | | | | | |
| # national FTE employees employed by service provider, as % of total | Total head count of supplier | Information submitted by vendor, e.g. upon contract award and/or with invoice | 1st tier | Commitments (award) or actuals (invoice) | CAPEX or OPEX | Good | Simple | Erroneous |
| # FTE national employees employed under contract, as % of total employees under contract | Head count under contract | Information submitted by vendor, e.g. upon contract award and/or with invoice | 1st tier | Commitments (award) or actuals (invoice) | CAPEX or OPEX | Moderate | Moderate | Erroneous |
| # FTE national employees in senior, supervisory and skilled positions (or other job or grade disaggregation) employed under contract, as % of employees under contract | Head count by job type | Information submitted by vendor, e.g. upon contract award and/or with invoice | 1st tier | Commitments (award) or actuals (invoice) | CAPEX or OPEX | Moderate | Moderate | Erroneous |
| # man-hours of FTE national employees under contract | Man-hours | Information submitted by vendor, e.g. upon contract award and/or with invoice | 1st and lower tiers | Commitments (award) or actuals (invoice) | CAPEX or OPEX | Moderate | Moderate | Proxy |
| $ value spent on with FTE national employees under contract as part of services contracted directly or indirectly (subcontracts), as % of total contract value | Wages | Information submitted by vendor, e.g. upon contract award and/or with invoice | 1st and lower tiers | Commitments (award) or actuals (invoice) | CAPEX or OPEX | Moderate | Moderate | Accurate |
| $ value of contracts on wages, social taxes and benefits to FTE national employees under contract, as % of total contract value | Build-up (stakeholder) method | Information submitted by vendor, e.g. at time of invoice | 1st and lower tiers | Commitments (award) or actuals (invoice) | CAPEX or OPEX | Poor | Complex | Accurate |
| As above, but for the set of largest contracts by value (e.g. top ten) | Largest contracts | Contracts Plan/information submitted by vendor | 1st and lower tiers | Commitments (award) or actuals (invoice) | CAPEX or OPEX | Moderate | Moderate | Accurate |

| Metric | Key feature | Information source | Supply chain penetration | Stage of procurement | Expenditure category | Confidence in data | Simplicity to administer | Economic accuracy* |
|---|---|---|---|---|---|---|---|---|
| $ value of contracts less proportion of contract value on salaries and bonuses (but not social taxes or expenses) of FTE foreign employees under contract, as % of contract value | Build-down method | Information submitted by vendor, e.g. at time of invoice | 1st and lower tiers | Commitments (award) or actuals (invoice) | CAPEX or OPEX | Moderate | Moderate | Accurate |
| As above, but for the set of largest contracts by value (e.g. top ten) | Largest contracts | Contracts Plan/information submitted by vendor | 1st and lower tiers | Commitments (award) or actuals (invoice) | CAPEX or OPEX | Good | Moderate | Accurate |
| **Goods-specific** | | | | | | | | |
| For suppliers and sub-suppliers certified as supplying goods of domestic origin, $ value of contracts for goods, as % of total expenditure | Step 1: domestic origin companies only. Step 2: all of contract value | Information submitted by vendor, e.g. upon contract award and/or with invoice | 1st and lower tiers | Commitments (award) or actuals (invoice) | CAPEX or OPEX | Poor/Good (depends on quality of certification) | Complex | Erroneous |
| For suppliers and sub-suppliers certified as supplying goods of domestic origin, proportion of $ value of contracts for goods retained in the domestic economy, as % of total expenditure | Step 1: domestic origin companies only. Step 2: portion of contract value retained in national economy | Information submitted by vendor, e.g. upon contract award and/or with invoice | 1st and lower tiers | Commitments (award) or actuals (invoice) | CAPEX or OPEX | Poor/Good (depends on quality of certification) | Complex | Proxy |
| $ value of contracts less proportion of imported components of purchased goods, e.g. cost-insurance-freight | Build-down method | Information submitted by vendor, e.g. upon contract award and/or with invoice | 1st and lower tiers | Commitments (award) or actuals (invoice) | CAPEX or OPEX | Moderate | Moderate | Accurate |
| As above, but for the set of largest contracts by value (e.g. top ten) | Largest contracts | Contracts Plan/information submitted by vendor | 1st and lower tiers | Commitments (award) or actuals (invoice) | CAPEX or OPEX | Good | Moderate | Accurate |

Table 9.2a **Typology of supplier development 'input' metrics**

| Metric | Key feature | Information source | Supply chain penetration | Stage of procurement | Expenditure category | Confidence in data | Simplicity to administer | Economic accuracy |
|---|---|---|---|---|---|---|---|---|
| **In-house** | | | | | | | | |
| # man-hours training for nationals, as % of total national man-hours | Training by man-hours | Human resources | n/a | n/a | OPEX | Good | Simple | Erroneous |
| # man-hours training for nationals on-the-job and in-the-classroom, as % of total national man-hours | Training by man-hours and by type | Human resources | n/a | n/a | OPEX | Good | Simple | Erroneous |
| $ value of training for nationals | Training by $ | Human resources | n/a | n/a | OPEX | Good | Simple | Proxy |
| $ value of training for nationals on-the-job and in-the-classroom | Training by $ and by training type | Human resources | n/a | n/a | OPEX | Good | Simple | Proxy |
| $ value of community contributions — vendor development and support programmes | Community vendor programmes | Information submitted by vendor, e.g. upon contract award and/ or with invoice | n/a | n/a | CAPEX or OPEX | Good | Simple | Proxy |
| $ value of community contributions — public infrastructure | Community infrastructure | Information submitted by vendor, e.g. upon contract award and/ or with invoice | n/a | n/a | CAPEX or OPEX | Good | Simple | Accurate |

| Metric | Key feature | Information source | Supply chain penetration | Stage of procurement | Expenditure category | Confidence in data | Simplicity to administer | Economic accuracy |
|---|---|---|---|---|---|---|---|---|
| **Contracted services and procured goods** | | | | | | | | |
| # man-hours on-the-job training for nationals under contract (including subcontractors), as % of total national man-hours under contract | Training by man-hours | Information submitted by vendor, e.g. upon contract award and/or with invoice | 1st tier | Commitments (award) or actuals (invoice) | CAPEX or OPEX | Moderate | Complex | Erroneous |
| # man-hours on-the-job training for nationals under contract (including subcontracts) on-the-job and in-the-classroom, as % of total national man-hours under contract | Training by man-hours and by type | Information submitted by vendor, e.g. upon contract award and/or with invoice | 1st tier | Commitments (award) or actuals (invoice) | CAPEX or OPEX | Poor | Complex | Erroneous |
| $ value of training for nationals under contract (including subcontractors) | Training by $ value | Information submitted by vendor, e.g. upon contract award and/or with invoice | 1st tier | Commitments (award) or actuals (invoice) | CAPEX or OPEX | Poor | Complex | Proxy |
| $ value of training for nationals under contract (including subcontracts) on-the-job and in-the-classroom | Training by $ value and by type | Information submitted by vendor, e.g. upon contract award and/or with invoice | 1st tier | Commitments (award) or actuals (invoice) | CAPEX or OPEX | Poor | Complex | Proxy |
| $ value of on-the-job management supervision and QA/QC to support nationally registered suppliers under contract (including subcontractors) | Management supervision and QA/QC | Information submitted by vendor, e.g. upon contract award and/or with invoice | 1st tier | Commitments (award) or actuals (invoice) | CAPEX or OPEX | Poor | Complex | Accurate |

| Metric | Key feature | Information source | Supply chain penetration | Stage of procurement | Expenditure category | Confidence in data | Simplicity to administer | Economic accuracy |
|---|---|---|---|---|---|---|---|---|
| $ of contract value as capital investments in enhancing the capabilities of nationally registered suppliers charged to parent company, as % of contract value | Capital investments to develop local suppliers—charged | Information submitted by vendor, e.g. upon contract award and/or with invoice | 1st tier | Commitments (award) or actuals (invoice) | CAPEX or OPEX | Moderate | Moderate | Accurate |
| $ capital investments in enhancing the capabilities of nationally registered suppliers not charged to parent company, as % of contract value | Capital investments to develop local suppliers—leveraged | Information submitted by vendor, e.g. upon contract award and/or with invoice | 1st tier | Commitments (award) or actuals (invoice) | CAPEX or OPEX | Moderate | Complex | Accurate |
| % of contract value as capital investments in dual-purpose infrastructure charged to parent company, as % of contract value | Dual-purpose infrastructure | Information submitted by vendor, e.g. upon contract award and/or with invoice | 1st tier | Commitments (award) or actuals (invoice) | CAPEX or OPEX | Moderate | Moderate | Accurate |

Table 9.2b **Typology of supplier development 'output' metrics**

| Metric | Key feature | Information source | Supply Chain Penetration | Stage of procurement | Expenditure Category | Confidence in data | Simplicity to administer | Economic accuracy |
|---|---|---|---|---|---|---|---|---|
| **Output metrics** | | | | | | | | |
| Contractor management performance (CPM) of nationally registered firms | CPM score cards for local suppliers/ contractors | Company CPM reports/company vendor register | 1st tier and lower tiers | Contractor performance management | CAPEX or OPEX | Moderate | Moderate | Accurate/ Proxy |
| % of tender lists comprising nationally registered suppliers (by different procurement categories) | Successful pre-qual/ tender lists | Company tender tracking system, e.g. PROCON | 1st tier | Commitments (award) or actuals (invoice) | CAPEX or OPEX | Good | Simple | Accurate |
| # contracts awarded to nationally registered vendors on an internationally competitive basis | Competitive contract award | Contracts plan/ company vendor register | 1st tier | Commitments (contract award) | CAPEX or OPEX | Good | Simple | Accurate |
| $ value of contracts awarded to nationally registered vendors on an internationally competitive basis | Competitive contract award | Contracts plan/ company vendor register | 1st tier | Commitments (contract award) | CAPEX or OPEX | Good | Simple | Accurate |
| # contracts awarded 'consequential' of supplier support from parent company | Contract award growth | Market survey | 1st and 2nd tier | n/a | CAPEX or OPEX | Moderate | Moderate | Proxy |
| $ of contracts awarded 'consequential' of supplier support from parent company | Revenue growth | Market survey | 1st and 2nd tier | n/a | CAPEX or OPEX | Poor | Moderate | Accurate |
| Reduction in price variance of labour rates or product prices between nationally registered suppliers and internationally competitive pricing | Price competitiveness improvements | Market survey | 1st tier and lower tiers | Contractor performance management | CAPEX or OPEX | Good/Poor (depends on quality of survey) | Complex | Accurate |

| Metric | Key feature | Information source | Supply Chain Penetration | Stage of procurement | Expenditure Category | Confidence in data | Simplicity to administer | Economic accuracy |
|---|---|---|---|---|---|---|---|---|
| Reduction in labour productivity variance between nationally registered suppliers and internationally competitive productivity | Labour productivity improvements | Market survey | 1st tier and lower tiers | Contractor performance management | CAPEX or OPEX | Good/Poor (depends on quality of survey) | Complex | Accurate |
| Reduction in defects rates variance between nationally registered suppliers and internationally competitive rates | Defect rates improvements | Market survey | 1st tier and lower tiers | Contractor performance management | CAPEX or OPEX | Good/Poor (depends on quality of survey) | Complex | Accurate |
| Improvement in HSE performance variance between nationally registered suppliers and internationally competitive HSE performance, e.g. lost-time injuries, total recordable incident frequency, first aid cases | HSE performance improvements | Market survey | 1st tier and lower tiers | Contractor performance management | CAPEX or OPEX | Good/Poor (depends on quality of survey) | Complex | Accurate |
| Improvement in volume/capacity variance between nationally registered suppliers and internationally competitive suppliers, e.g. maximum crane tonnage lift, maximum fabrication yard area, maximum piping storage volume | Volume/ capacity improvements | Market survey | 1st tier and lower tiers | Contractor performance management | CAPEX or OPEX | Good/Poor (depends on quality of survey) | Complex | Accurate |

A comparison of selected metrics from the two tables follows, ana-lysed from the following perspectives: their key features; the stage of procurement at which they apply; the relevant expenditure catego-ries; confidence in the data; simplicity to administer; and economic accuracy.

# In-house local content: headcount vs. wage value

A simple measure of local content within a development or operat-ing company is the number of nationals employed as a proportion of total full-time equivalent (FTE) employees. Such a metric is com-mon in concession agreements[3] to define local content targets for national professional and non-professional staff. The targets derived from this metric may include anticipated performance over time: for example, 70% of nationals in managerial positions in year one of the concession, and 90% in year five. A variant on headcount is to report the proportion of total man hours of work undertaken by national citizens in different job types or grades.

With headcount metrics, ambiguity can arise in the definition of both 'nationals' and 'employees'. One rule of thumb is to include individuals who have national citizenship and are on the company payroll, thus including full- and part-time agency staff.

An alternative to headcount as a measure of in-house local content is to measure the actual value paid by the company to employees and other payrolled staff. Most usual is to use a gross wage or gross salary measure. This metric combines base salary, associated social taxes paid by employee and employer, and employee benefits and

---

3  The term 'concession agreement' is used in a generalised sense to mean any agreement made between a state and company for the exploration or development of mining resources (metals, minerals, oil or gas) in which the state offers incentives, such as exclusivity to seek profit, reduced tax or royalty rates, cost recovery or production-sharing arrangements, in exchange for long-term capital investment in the country.

expenses, including pension contributions, housing, personal and vehicle allowances, and bonuses.

Both headcount and gross wage metrics are relatively simple to administer, calculated as they are from information already collected by human resources and financial accounts departments. As such, confidence in these data should also be reasonably high.

These attributes are important, but as reliable measures of economic value contributed to the domestic economy, both metrics are prone to a number of inaccuracies as follows.

Headcount, when used to report local content in expenditure on human resources in a company that uses expat labour, can be particularly misleading. For example, it would not be unusual for the headcount of national citizens in an oil and gas operating company to be 85% across all grades, but accounting for only 15% of the total payroll bill (plus social taxes and benefits).

The common answer to this problem is to report gross salary paid to national citizens, as introduced above. But this too can be misleading. Although expatriate base salaries are often paid into foreign bank accounts, and thus accumulate overseas, expat allowances for housing, transport and personal expenses, as well as expat social taxes, will accrue to the domestic economy. These expenditures should not be underestimated. In one anonymous economic assessment of local content in the upstream oil sector undertaken by the author, the in-country allowances and social taxes paid to and on behalf of expatriates were three times the total gross wages and social taxes paid to and on behalf of all national citizens in the same company.[4]

When discussing in-house metrics for local content, an important distinction needs to be drawn between the mining and oil and gas development sectors. Whereas a few hundred to a thousand FTE employees would be typical in an oil or gas development or operating company, in the mining sector, these figures can be ten times larger, depending on the extent to which labour to operate the mines is in-house or subcontracted.

4  Refer to author: mwarner@localcontentsolutions.com.

## Defining 'local' supplier

Regarding the reporting of local content within procurement expenditure, a controversial topic is what is meant by a 'local' supplier.[5] Common definitions include:

- The address given in vendor registration information

- The address on a purchase order or invoice

- The share of equity owned by nationals, e.g. > 50%

- Whether the supplier is incorporated in-country

- Whether the supplier is tax-registered in-country, e.g. for corporate tax or withholding tax

- Whether the supplier is a producer or provider of goods or services of 'domestic origin' (see below)

With regard to regional or community suppliers, more refined definitions can include:

- Regional/local address in vendor registration

- Regional/local address on invoice

- Suppliers and contractors who source the majority of materials or labour from the province, district or local communities located closest to the operation

In establishing such metrics, the regulator or company is then left with the choice of whether to require reporting of the **number** of such suppliers or the **$ value** of expenditure.

Probably the metric that is most time-consuming to define, and most prone to error, is where a local supplier is described by the proportion of equity owned by national citizens. In theory, information on equity share is readily forthcoming through investigation of annual financial accounts, websites and the state office of company incorporation. Yet in practice few operating companies are willing

---

5  Unless otherwise indicated, the term 'supplier' is used in its general sense to describe all types of vendor, including suppliers of goods under a purchase order or agreement, and suppliers of services under contract.

to invest the resources involved to undertake this type of detailed research.

Furthermore, there are few opportunities for short cuts here. For example, it cannot be assumed that a supplier who is incorporated within the country is necessarily majority-owned by nationals; nor can it be assumed that a supplier incorporated in a foreign country is not majority owned by nationals. In general, then, such realities prohibit regulators from accurately reporting to politicians the extent to which nationally owned firms are participating in procurement.

Measuring local content as equity participation is far from being the only source of potential error in this class of metric. Defining a 'local' supplier by applying the company address in vendor registration information, or from a purchase order or invoice, is administratively simply, but carries even greater potential for inaccuracy, if intended to convey how much expenditure is retained in the domestic economy.

Inaccuracies in using the office address are more likely when reporting on the purchase of goods than the contracting of services. With goods, especially finished manufactured equipment and materials, a local address on an invoice may simply reflect the office location of an importing agent. These agents (the so-called 'Mr 10%s') are often wholly indigenous and reliable suppliers of equipment and materials, but the goods involved are essentially imported. The proportion of the sales price retained in the domestic economy comprises only the commission paid to the agent and the import duties. Even if the import agent offers additional services, such as storage and in-land freight, a company reporting 100% local content for these goods on the basis that the supplier's office is located in-county, is reporting information that is potentially misleading.

To illustrate how misleading such reporting can be, Figure 9.3 compares how local content might be reported for a hypothetical purchase of spare parts and their fitting and testing.

In the example, a purchase order for US$4 million has been raised for the supply of machine spare parts under a call-off contract. Two scenarios are compared. In the first, the supplier's main office is located in-country. This supplier imports goods that are already finished and packaged. He provides a storage facility, and transports

Figure 9.3 **Misleading nature of certain local content metrics**

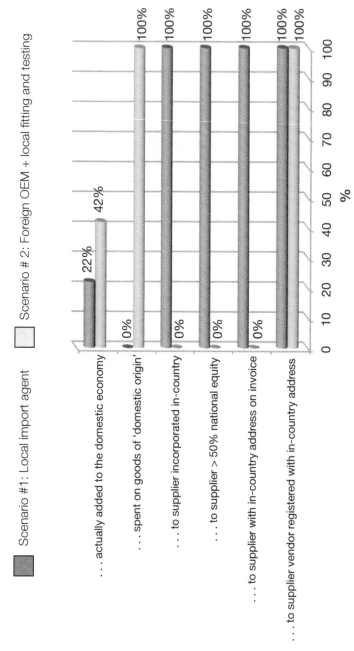

the parts on demand to the end user. Fitting and testing services are performed through a subcontract between the agent and the foreign original equipment manufacturer (OEM).

In a second scenario, the supplier's main office is located overseas, but he has made recent investment in local capability to store, transport, fit and test the parts. These in-country capabilities contribute 42% of the actual total purchase agreement. The goods are deemed by regulators to be of 'domestic origin' because more than 40% of the value of the sales has originated in-country.

Figure 9.3 clearly shows how inaccuracies can arise from reporting local content using simple metrics such as country address on key documentation. In both scenarios each scores 100% local content with respect to the in-country location of the suppliers' main office as recorded in the company's vendor registration database. But with regard to using the address on an invoice, the supplier in scenario 2, who is invoicing from its overseas office, records 0% local content, while the local import agent in scenario 1 scores 100%. The same inverse relationship occurs with equity ownership, where the supplier in scenario 1 is 100% owned by nationals, and in scenario 2 is 100% foreign-owned.

And the ambiguities run deeper still. With respect to measuring local content in terms of goods of 'domestic origin', in scenario 2 all of the purchase agreement value is counted as local content because the proportion of this agreement assumed to be of domestic origin is greater than the threshold of 40%. This is so, despite only 42% of the actual purchase agreement price staying in the domestic economy.

In contrast, in scenario 1, although 22% of the contract value stays in the domestic economy as a combination of commission to the agent and payment for storage and freight costs, local content is reported as 0% because 22% is below the 40% threshold for goods to be defined as being of domestic origin.

## Importance of description and context

Figure 9.3 demonstrates how different local content metrics can not only generate relatively different results, but also lead to diametrically opposite conclusions. What is crucial, then, is for the statements and messages communicated around these data to be a true and fair interpretation of the measurement in question.

To illustrate, the following statement: 'We spent US$950 million on procurement this year, of which 47% was local content' is not altogether uncommon in company reports. The statement is, however, rather meaningless if reported without clarity on the definition of local content being used, and what is meant by the term 'spent'. Reporting aggregate figures for local content in this way also raises the question of how the 47% figure is spread between operational and capital expenditure and across different expenditure categories. Table 9.3 gives the actual information upon which this generalised statement might have been based.

Table 9.3 **Illustrative data on local content**

| | **Year 2010** | | |
| | **US$ millions total** | **US$ spent with suppliers tax-registered in-country (US$ millions)** | **Local content (%)** |
|---|---|---|---|
| **Committed expenditure (contract awarded)** | | | |
| Services | 700 | 425 | 61 |
| Goods | 250 | 22 | 9 |
| Total | 950 | 447 | 47 |
| **Actual expenditure (invoiced)** | | | |
| Services | 450 | 280 | 62 |
| Goods | 130 | 55 | 42 |
| Total | 580 | 335 | 58 |

The data in Table 9.3 are sufficient to support a far more meaningful statement than in the previous communication, for example:

> In 2010, US$950 million was committed for expenditure on goods and services, of which US$447 million (47%) was awarded to suppliers tax-registered in-country. Of this US$447 million, US$425 is for the future provision of local

services, and US$22 million for the future supply of goods from local suppliers. The relatively low figure of US$22 million is explained by the period of capital refurbishment anticipated for 2011. A more routine figure for standard operations would be around 40%, as evidenced by actual expenditure against invoices from local tax-registered suppliers in 2010.

When reporting local content, it is far safer and clearer to precisely communicate the metric being applied and, where necessary, provide context so that the real trends are transparent. As a rule of thumb: avoid using the term 'local content' when reporting local content, and instead just say what it is that you mean.

# Rules of origin and local content

A suite of more complex metrics for local content derives from rules of origin. Rules of origin are the principles applied to determine whether a product is eligible for preferential treatment in trade. These rules are now being applied by some regulators to design local content targets and reporting requirements. The same rules have also informed the local content metrics used in the investment criteria of national development banks: for example, the 60% local content requirement of the Brazilian national development bank, BNDES, for extending finance for fixed investments in machinery and equipment.[6] In turn, these investment criteria have influenced local content reporting regulations, most notably in Brazil and Mexico.

Rules of origin have and continue to be debated at length by the World Trade Organisation, the European Union, NAFTA (North American Free Trade Agreement) and governments in bilateral trade agreements and negotiations. Common points of contention are the methods and thresholds for determining whether an imported prod-

---

6 S. Robert, *National Development Banks in Sustainable Financing: Addressing Market Failures* (Johannesburg: Competition Commission and the University of Witwatersrand, 2007).

uct has undergone what is termed a 'substantive transformation' in-country, such that the good is eligible for trade preferences.

One such determinant is the level of 'value addition' achieved in the exporting country. Generally the methods for calculating value addition are one of two types: 'build-up' methods and 'build-down' methods. The distinction here is important, and lies at the heart of much of the current discourse on the ambiguities and administrative complexities of local content reporting.

'Build-up' methods aggregate, piecemeal, the value added to the domestic economy from in-country industrial activity, essentially the cost of labour and direct manufacturing costs, but excluding the cost of imported materials.

If one applies the logic of 'build-up' methods to the gross salary metric reviewed earlier in this chapter, this would suggest adding the base salary of nationals to employer and employee tax contributions and employee benefits of nationals, and then also adding in the allowances and benefits paid to expats (but excluding expat base salaries and bonuses). In other words, the figure for local content is 'built up' from the individual local components.

In contrast, 'build-down' methods seek to identify the non-originating—foreign—content, then deduct this from the overall transaction price. Continuing with the above example, a 'build-down' method applied to measure in-house local content would take the entire employee wage bill and all taxes and benefits as the starting point, and then deduct that portion paid to expats as base salary and bonuses. This would theoretically leave the originating value being contributed to the domestic economy, i.e. the proportion that is local content.

Under rules of origin for trade preferences, there then takes place a critical second step. A threshold is applied to the originating portion (whether this is derived from a build-up or build-down method). This threshold is the point at which a good is considered to have undergone 'substantive transformation' in-country. The critical rule is that trade preferences are then applied to the entire transaction value of the exported good, not only the proportion that is of domestic origin.

The significance of this second step in reporting local content in oil and gas expenditure is demonstrated by the different ways in which examples of formulae from Brazil and Kazakhstan have utilised rules of origin methods (refer to Table 9.4). In the Brazil example, both steps in the process are followed as a 'build-down' method to calculate local content in goods and services. In the Kazakhstan example, the formula for reporting local content applies the first step of calculating domestic origin, but not the second step, with a 'build-up' method used for goods and a 'build-down' method for services.

It is not altogether clear why in the Brazil example the formula uses the two-step process applicable under rules of origin. Since there is no tangible trade advantage to achieving some arbitrary threshold of 'substantive transformation', there is no obvious reason for assuming that goods that are over 40% domestic origin should be reported as 100% local content. Indeed, other formulae used in the Brazil oil and gas industry forgo this second step.

Table 9.4 **Metrics to measure goods and services of domestic origin: comparison of Brazil and Kazakhstan**

Sources: Brazilian Local Content Requirements, undated (assumed 2009); Republic of Kazakhstan, General Provisions: Single Methodology to Calculate Kazakhstani Content Pertaining to Purchased Goods, Works and Services, September 2009.

| An example from Brazil | An example from Kazakhstan |
| --- | --- |
| **Step 1: Calculate % local content in goods and services** ||
| **Screening of components for evaluation**<br><br>Subset of components subjected to evaluation, based on Pareto's 80/20 rule (inputs ranked by value) with remaining 20% and certain goods assumed to be 100% Brazilian without need for evaluation<br><br>**Build-down method: Nationalisation Index for Goods (INB)**<br><br>*[Sales price] less [value of direct and third-party imported components as FOB (or CIF) and import duties]*<br><br>―――――――――<br><br>*Sales price*<br><br>Correction factor to take account of overheads incurred outside Brazil<br><br>**Build-down method: Nationalisation Index for Services (INS)**<br><br>*[Service price] less [Imported human resources (value of foreign man hours) +*<br><br>*Imported capital goods used to provide services (rental, leasing) +*<br><br>*Intermediary imported goods/ consumables]*<br><br>―――――――――<br><br>*Service price* | **Build-down method: local content metrics for goods (used in calculation of CT-KZ Certificate of Origin)**<br><br>*'Cost of the foreign raw material and other components'*<br><br>―――――――――<br><br>*Sales price*<br><br>This metric is only applied in the context of calculating the % domestic figure in preparation of a CT-KZ Certificate confirming that goods are produced in the Republic of Kazakhstan<br><br>**Build-up method: local content metric for services**<br><br>*(CT-KZ % in goods used to provide services)*<br>*+*<br>*(Share of salary fund by citizens of Kazakhstan pursuant to primary contract)*<br>*+*<br>*(Value of subcontracts performed by legal entities of RoK with > 95% national citizens)*<br><br>―――――――――<br><br>*Service price* |

| An example from Brazil | An example from Kazakhstan |
|---|---|
| **Step 2: Classification of local content as goods or services of domestic origin** | |
| Goods and services origin verification | Goods of Origin Certification |
| **Goods**<br>If INB >40%, then goods are 100% Brazilian, and total sales price counts towards local content targets<br><br>**Services**<br>If INS >80% then services are 100% Brazilian, and total service price counts towards local content targets | **Goods**<br>% share of Kazakh content in goods, as specified in the CT-KZ Certificate<br><br>If there is no CT-KZ Certificate of Origin, Kazakh content is 0%, regardless |

Arguably, the central tenet of reporting local content in procurement expenditure is to communicate the value being contributed by this expenditure to the domestic economy. As such, the single step approach being adopted in Kazakhstan would seem more credible.

With regard to the choice of 'build-up' versus 'build-down' methods, in both Brazil and Kazakhstan reporting regulations require use of a 'build-down' method to calculate local content in goods. In Brazil, the metric involves deducting the 'CIF' Incoterm (cost, insurance, freight) dollar figure from the sales price, along with import taxes and overseas overhead costs. In Kazakhstan, the same principles are at play, but the precise metric remains unclear.

The main difference in choice of methods is in the calculation of local content for the contracting of services. In Brazil, the method is to build downwards: that is, to deduct the foreign labour component from the total contract price. In Kazakhstan, at the time of writing, the applicable method was to identify the gross salary and benefits of nationals utilised in contract delivery, and add this to the total value of subcontracts awarded to those nationally registered service providers with greater than 95% of national employees, by headcount: in other words, a build-up method.

# Incoterms and local content

International commerce terms (Incoterms) are published by the International Chamber of Commerce and widely used in international transactions.[7] The core Incoterms relevant to calculating the non-originating component of procurement expenditure on goods under a 'build-down' method are 'FOB' (free on board) and 'CIF' (cost, insurance, freight).

In calculating local content, if a supplier has paid for goods FOB, then the subsequent port-to-port freight costs and associated insurance would need to be added to the FOB price before deducting this from the total sales price. This explains why CIF is favoured as the metric for calculating local content under a 'build-down' method, since CIF includes the non-originating costs up to the port of entry. Figures 9.4 and 9.5 compare how FOB with CIF can be used in the calculation of local content.

Figure 9.4 **Goods paid as FOB**

Source: adapted from Wikipedia; en.wikipedia.org/wiki/Incoterm

Seller – Carrier – Frontier – Harbour – Harbour – Customs – Buyer

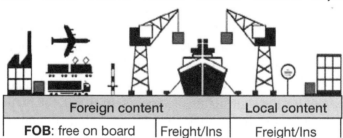

| Foreign content | | Local content |
|---|---|---|
| **FOB**: free on board | Freight/Ins | Freight/Ins |

---

7  For a full description of Incoterms, see Wikipedia; en.wikipedia.org/wiki/ Incoterm, accessed 9 February 2011.

Figure 9.5 **Goods paid as CIF**

Source: adapted from Wikipedia; en.wikipedia.org/wiki/Incoterm

Seller – Carrier – Frontier – Harbour – Harbour – Customs – Buyer

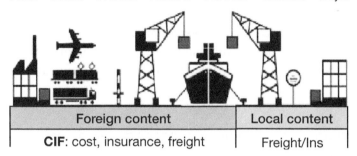

The attraction of using a 'build-down' method to calculate, especially if derived from **FOB** or **CIF** Incoterms, is their relative administrative simplicity. FOB and CIF information is identifiable in the buyer's internal documentation, and can readily be deducted from total sales price to generate a reasonably accurate figure for local content.[8] This said, there is a not insignificant drawback to using Incoterms to calculate local content. Invariably, reporting local content using FOB and CIF means suppliers are asked to disclose the results of their price negotiations with sellers: information that can be commercially sensitive. In Brazil, this limitation is being addressed through an independent third-party system of certification, with local content reported on an aggregated basis.

## Measuring supplier development

With reference to the first myth discussed at the beginning of this chapter, higher levels of local content do not necessarily imply that a country or region's industrial base is becoming stronger or more competitive. While it may indeed mean that more direct and indirect

---

8 It is assumed that the proportion of sales price for foreign overheads is not material.

jobs are being created, and local order books look more healthy, these data say little about whether national employees or local suppliers and service contractors are developing their capabilities and capacity and as a result wining more work and growing as long-term, viable businesses.

Metrics that measure the 'development' of local suppliers are equally diverse as those available to measure 'content'. These metrics can be divided into two categories: input metrics and output metrics.

## Input metrics for measuring supplier development

Input metrics are essentially proxy indicators for measures of outcome or performance. For example, a development or operating company would expect the future earning power of employees who have received vocational training, or the future growth prospects of community-based suppliers who have benefited from vendor development programmes, to be at least equal to the cost of providing the training or delivering the programmes.

Likewise, levels of capital investment in local suppliers to build capability made by an operating company, or leveraged from international contractors or third-party financial institutions, can also be claimed as a proxy indicator for the growth potential of these suppliers.

These are the most simple supplier development metrics, and, as is discussed in Chapter 5, may have a role to play in the evaluation of tenders as a means to incentivise lead contractors to support and develop local suppliers.

## Output metrics for measuring supplier development

Output metrics to measure local supplier development are more meaningful but, to date, companies have had difficulty in identifying metrics that are sufficiently robust and yet simple and resource-efficient to administer.

Most robust would be those that measure actual improvements over time in the core parameters of firm competitiveness, for example:

- Supplier costs

- Delivery times

- Labour productivity

- Quality, including defect rates

- Volume capacity

- HSE performance

To calibrate performance, these results obtained would need to be benchmarked against international norms. Such metrics can be applied, but require a significant commitment of resources in order to undertake the necessary surveys at the level of individual suppliers. One efficiency measure here would be to combine this type of survey with conventional market testing, for example, when preparing for a new capital project.

Other useful output metrics, equally dependent on local market surveys, are to investigate what new contracts local suppliers have won as a result of being contracted by, or supplying to, the oil, gas or mining company in question, and how their revenues have grown over time as a result. Positive trends in these two metrics would be meaningful since they demonstrate whether local suppliers are becoming more competitive and growing. However, confidence in the results would need to be predicated on a clear cause-and-effect linkage between the new contracts being won and the vendor support programmes of the company and its lead contractors.

Believability in the data would be less where evidence that local firms are becoming more marketable and expanding their business is only partially linked to having been contracted to the company in question: that is, where the bulk of new revenues have actually come from contracts or orders executed for clients more widely.

## Missing metrics

These are not inconsequential limitations, and there is clearly a need for simpler metrics that negate the need for resource-intensive surveys or proof of a cause-and-effect linkage. One set of alternatives is for the oil, gas or mining company to report on trends in the number and type of local suppliers who:

- Make it through pre-qualification processes

- Are selected for tender lists

- Are awarded contracts on an internationally competitive basis

These three metrics can work well as indicators of successful local supplier development, but only if there is an open internationally competitive tendering process in operation and no anticompetitive preferencing of local suppliers (for example, through cost advantages or excessive targets). In such cases a positive trend in the numbers and value of local suppliers making it through pre-qualification or being awarded contracts on an internationally competitive basis, would be solid evidence that local industry is becoming more competitive.

These would seem to be helpful and administratively efficient metrics. Yet few regulators require companies to report against them, and few companies disclose this information on a voluntary basis. These missing metrics can be summarised as follows:

1. **Competitive pre-qualification**. % of vendors in master subcontractor lists and tender lists that comprise nationally registered suppliers (by different procurement categories). Data source: company tender tracking system, e.g. PROCON

2. **Competitive contract award**. # and $ value of contracts awarded to nationally registered vendors on an internationally competitive basis. Data source: contracts plan/company vendor register

# Conclusions

This chapter has sought to demonstrate that the choice of metrics for measuring and reporting local content in oil, gas and mining expenditure is large and the potential ambiguities involved in their application many.

Some of the emergent principles for accurate and efficient reporting are as follows:

- Report both relative and absolute figures, to avoid communicating misleading information

- If there are ambiguities due to changing metrics, report two sets of data using the old and new metrics

- As far as possible disaggregate the information reported, so that low or high levels of local content are not hidden within aggregate figures

- Accurately describe the metrics being used to generate the reported figures, and not only the figures themselves

- Report the total data population that is the basis for reporting, alongside the proportion of expenditure not included in this population

- Beware applying rules of origin without adaptation; these were designed for a different purpose

# Index

Page numbers in *italic figures* refer to figures and tables;
the abbreviation LC is used for 'local content'.

# About the author

 Dr Michael Warner has 22 years of experience aligning business strategy with the socioeconomic priorities of host countries. He is the former architect of BG Group's standards and procurement-based procedures for local content management, and the Group's risk-based approach to supply chain sustainability. He is also former Co-ordinator for the Oil, Gas and Mining Secretariat of the World Bank programme on Business Partners for Development, and a former Research Fellow with the Overseas Development Institute managing the Business and Development programme. Currently Director of the specialist training and consultancy firm Local Content Solutions (LCS), he has worked in Europe, Africa, Central and South-East Asia, the Middle East and Latin America, and on assignments for BP, Shell, BG Group, World Bank, IFC, DFID, UNDP, FAO, WEF, Anglo American, Alcan, Newmont Mining, AMEC, Balfour Beatty, Sodexho and others.

For Product Safety Concerns and Information please contact our EU
representative GPSR@taylorandfrancis.com Taylor & Francis Verlag GmbH,
Kaufingerstraße 24, 80331 München, Germany


Printed and bound by CPI Group (UK) Ltd, Croydon, CR0 4YY

01/05/2025

01858460-0001